Pictorial Continuity

How to shoot a movie story

By ARTHUR L. GASKILL

and DAVID A. ENGLANDER

Photographs and drawings by Irving Levine
Former instructor, Army Photographic School

Essential Books

DUELL, SLOAN AND PEARCE
New York

I

PREFACE

In early 1942, during the darkest days of Axis military supremacy, the War Department called upon the Signal Corps Photographic Center to train motion-picture photographers to record the great Allied offensives of the future.

The armed forces were scoured for potential combat cameramen, but only a handful of soldiers who had motion-picture experience—either as professionals or amateurs—was discovered. Most students were men with still-camera experience only, or raw beginners who regarded moving-picture apparatus with the same uncertainty as an infernal machine.

Hastily trained in a seventeen-week course, sometimes called abruptly from their uncompleted studies and ordered overseas, these Signal Corps photographers nevertheless acquitted themselves with skill, sureness, and lasting though anonymous glory. Their combat films of Allied campaigns from North Africa to Okinawa were seen in every theatre of the country, and were the nucleus of the great documentaries of this war. *The True Glory, San Pietro, Attack Signal,* and *Appointment in Tokyo* are testimonials to the courage of the Army photographer—and to the effectiveness of the training he received.

What were the ingredients of that training, so hurried and often so incomplete, which can explain the success of comparative beginners?

Solid grounding in camera mechanics like loading, focus, and exposure, was basic, but the real secret lay in the teaching of the technique of *how* to shoot a motion-picture story.

It was a technique that brought with it new terms and new ideas which were so logical they seemed obvious facts once they had been pointed out. It was a technique without which a real motion picture could *not* be made, regardless of mechanical precision. It was a technique essential to every production, whether Hollywood epic, newsreel, documentary, cartoon, or homemade movie of the baby in her crib.

That technique is the subject of our book. We know it as PICTORIAL CONTINUITY.

CONTENTS

vii

Pictorial Continuity

How to shoot a movie story

CHAPTER ONE

PICTORIAL CONTINUITY:
THE SIMPLE SEQUENCE

THE MEANING OF CONTINUITY

Most people who have pressed the button of either a still or a movie camera appreciate the fact that a motion picture is only a series of still pictures in which the change between the frames is so slight that the illusion of motion is gained.

But a good motion picture is more than just a series of animated snapshots. It hangs together, it tells a story smoothly, coherently, logically. The know-how of this is contained in the technique of *pictorial continuity*.

Pictorial continuity is a rather fancy term, but we like it, because it states so precisely what we're out to describe. The dictionary explains "continuity" as an "uninterrupted, close union of separate parts." Pictorial continuity, therefore, in a fully rounded definition, would be *the proper development and connection of motion-picture sequences to create a smoothly joined, coherent motion-picture story.*

BASIC ELEMENTS OF THE SEQUENCE

Defining more closely, we use the dictionary description of a "sequence" as a "series of things following in a certain order or succession," and we therefore term our motion-picture sequence a *related series of shots*. The sequence thus is a fundamental unit in pictorial continuity. And it has three simple basic elements: the long shot, the medium shot, and the closeup. We break down the sequence this way because all people view action in real life with their eyes in terms of long shot, medium shot, and closeup, even if they do not realize it.

Grasp these elements, and their correct, logical use, and you have caught the basic idea. They are elementary, but you cannot start without learning them. They are the ABC's of continuity; the XYZ's will come in due time.

THE LONG SHOT

We say these elements are simple and that they correspond to the stages by which the human eye views action. Let's prove it by shooting a simple sequence.

We will use two admirable photographic instruments. First, we'll shoot with the greatest, most inimitable camera of them all—the human eye. Then we'll shoot the same action with a motion-picture camera.

Now for our action. We want something ordinary and everyday, such as one person's visiting another. To bring it closer to home, we make it an event which has doubtless occurred in the lives of many of our readers

—profitably, we trust, for some: a salesman's call on a prospective customer.

You enter the door of Mr. Prospect's office. The scene is new to you, so you hesitate for an instant to orient yourself and to satisfy your curiosity. *Your eye has automatically started to shoot.* In a split-second glance, it has swept the room, registering walls, ceiling, window, charts, desk, and most important, Mr. Prospect seated at the telephone. Your eye, in short, has established the locale and your subject in it.

Now your camera must do for a movie audience what your eye did for you, so that what the audience sees on the screen will be what your eye has seen in real life, so that it will know without asking questions that it is looking at an office.

This first shot which *establishes the scene* is the *long shot,* the "LS."

Well, then, take it. Pick up your camera and, guided by what your eye sees in the viewfinder, shoot.

Don't move your camera so fast! Shoot what your eye sees, but don't try to shoot it *in the same way.* There's no camera made that can imitate your eye in throwing a glance around the room with lightning speed. Try it with your camera and you'll have a weird, waving effect (blurred, too, if you do it fast enough) that will force your audience to shut its eyes because it is so painful to look at.

Many an over-ambitious but under-experienced beginner has lost his audience by selling his photographic soul for a "flashy pan." You'll have an excuse to "pan" later—on the right occasion.

Right now, your LS can be taken from a nice, steady, stationary position. From where you stand in the doorway, you are far enough back to take in your subject and a great deal of his surroundings—enough to establish the locale.

If you are fussy about composition, you can move back even more, and shoot the office interior with the doorway as a frame on either side. It won't be worth it, though, if you cut off too much of the interior, or if your subject is so far away that he seems lost. It is, after all, *his* office; *he* dominates *it*. You don't want to suggest the reverse. This is just a simple homemade movie, not a psychological drama by Orson Welles.

By now, the long shot and its function should be well established in your mind. Go on into the office, with your eye again doing the shooting.

You and your eye want to get as close to your subject as you can. As you move in toward Mr. Prospect, your eye instantly, automatically, and continuously keeps readjusting itself to the changing perspective and proportions of the scene. It takes in increasingly more and more of Mr. Prospect, his face, hair, shoulders, tie, shirt, the articles on his desk, and less and less of the rest of his surroundings, such as the wall, the window, and the body of the desk.

This is the way you want it. After all, the vital part of the scene is Mr. Prospect, not his location. You want to cut out as much of the extraneous, distracting locale as you can, and come as close to his face as your eye, and politeness, will allow. This is your closeup, the heart of your picture.

THE MEDIUM SHOT

But before discussing the closeup, we must look at the technique by which we duplicate the eye's transition from long shot to closeup with the camera. This brings forth the inevitable question. Why is a transition shot needed at all?

The argument is as follows: We say that the closeup is the heart of the picture. We take the LS, which no one disputes is essential for background. So, once the scene is established, why waste the audience's time and the photographer's film on a transition shot, why not go *directly* to the closeup?

It is a good question, but one which overlooks a vital factor. Never forget that your camera is mimicking the human eye. Suppose you were suddenly blindfolded as you stood at the door of Mr. Prospect's office; then his charming secretary took you by the hand, led you right up to him, and abruptly removed the blindfold so that you found yourself staring at Mr. Prospect within a foot of his face. What would your reaction be?

You would certainly be lost momentarily. The jump from the general long shot to the intimate, concentrated closeup would have been too much for the eye. Instinctively, it would seek to reorient itself by looking around the room and again placing Mr. Prospect in relation to his surroundings.

Now suppose an audience, looking at your film on the screen, is suddenly confronted with that closeup after seeing the long shot. It cannot look around the room, outside the boundaries of the screen, to orient itself. Imagine how much greater the shock would be for it!

No, this great jump will not do. It is too abrupt. There must be a midway or transition shot—the *medium shot*.

What do you do then—mimic the eye as it moves from long shot to closeup by grinding away constantly with your camera as you move in on Mr. Prospect? That would be wasteful, tedious, and give a very jumpy picture, unless you used a "dolly" (a stable platform mounted on wheels) which would keep your camera steady as it moved. But that's a rather elaborate gadget, and what is more important, it's unnecessary.

One stationary shot about midway will be perfectly adequate. By moving closer to your subject, you eliminate a lot of background detail no longer of interest. What is more, your subject grows larger on the screen; interest is being concentrated on him; and smoothly, naturally, unobtrusively, he is being built up for the ultimate closeup.

The medium shot, or "MS," is *a transition shot bridging the jump from long shot to closeup, and building up the subject.*

Before proceeding, it is essential to clear up any uncertainty about just *where* to place the MS. We called it a midway shot, but that term, like so many others in motion-picture photography, is elastic. The medium shot does not have to be a mathematical half of the distance between long shot and closeup. It can be nearer either one, whichever serves the purpose better. It depends on the circumstances; long shot, medium shot,

Long Shot

Medium Shot

Closeup

THE SIMPLE SEQUENCE: Basic Elements

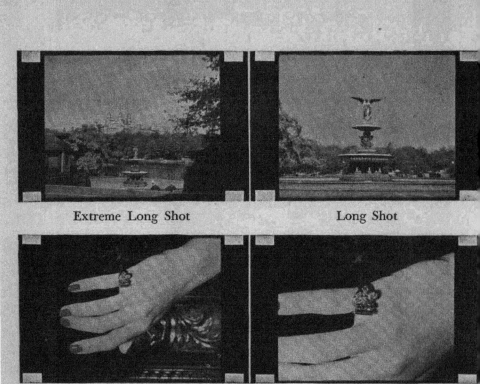

Extreme Long Shot   Long Shot

Closeup   Extreme Closeup

Three examples of the
Full-Figure Shot

and closeup are all relative. Bear in mind only that you want your transition to be smooth, and your subject to be built up gradually.

For the case in point, an MS taking in the top of Mr. Prospect's desk and a little of the background suits your purpose nicely. The desk is now not just another piece of furniture, but the main prop to set off—and focus attention on—Mr. Prospect.

THE CLOSEUP

It is the *closeup*, the "CU," to which the LS and MS, properly executed, pave the way.

Your human eye, we noted, came as close to Mr. Prospect as it could. And that closeness created intimacy and warmth. Your eye's CU gratified a natural urge to see Mr. Prospect from a point where his facial expressions might be studied closely and in detail.

Thus when your camera takes its closeup your audience will see Mr. Prospect's face, his head and shoulders filling the screen, his every expression vivid and alive. In the full meaning of the term, he will be "big as life." Certain things about him that might have been vague or lost to the audience in a long or medium shot —his prominent nose, his dapper mustache, his fancy tie—all elements of his personality will now strike the audience with great emphasis and clarity. It, too, will be face to face with Mr. Prospect and be able to observe and respond to the play of emotion his face shows. The closeup is the most revealing, the most expressive of motion-picture shots.

The use of the CU can be a great art; its mere introduction by David Wark Griffith revolutionized early film technique. So don't take it for granted, or dismiss it as obvious. It is obvious enough when seen, but many years of movie-making passed before Griffith first used it.

It is sadly neglected by the home movie cameraman today.

ACTION—NOT POSING!

There is a word we have used with great familiarity, a word describing something so inherent in motion-picture continuity, so much taken for granted that it is often passed by without proper mention. The word is *action*. Let us hold onto it for a moment and give it due emphasis.

It is a characteristic of the animated-snapshot, pseudo-movie to have the subjects *posing*, doing nothing but obviously waiting to have their picture taken, obviously aware of what is going on.

Now, pictorial continuity must create a motion-picture *story*. To achieve the effect of a story, get your subjects to *do* something; don't let them stand or sit stiffly and stare into the camera.

(The very bad thing about staring into the camera is that the audience immediately perceives that the actor is *aware* of the camera. This destroys that enjoyable illusion of being privileged to peep into a scene wherein the players are unconscious of spectators; it destroys the scene's naturalness.)

Getting a subject *to do something* is very simple. Instead of leaving Mr. Prospect just sitting there, waiting to "have his picture took," give him something to do. Have him use the phone, or write a note, or both. Even though he may sit motionless as he listens intently to the phone, his attitude *suggests* action.

Giving your subject a natural action to perform relaxes him, diverts his attention from the camera, and makes the scene appear to be "stolen" directly from life.

AUDIENCE REACTION

It cannot be too stubbornly reiterated that the photographer must enable his audience to see action on the screen the same way he sees it with his own eye. Always the cameraman must remember the screen's limitations, must remember that the audience is at the mercy of the screen. He must keep that audience at all times clearly informed of what is going on through what the film depicts. In other words, action should be self-explanatory. Sound and dialogue may be added as trimmings, but never as *necessities.*

You cannot be too greatly preoccupied with audience reaction. If you are going to show your films to friends, neighbors, and relatives, to local camera clubs, you've got to be concerned with it. You must never assume that they will know the things you unconsciously take for granted.

If you plan to take pictures of Baby cavorting in her playpen why, you may ask, waste good film on long and medium shots to establish a room already familiar to you through a thousand comings and goings? Why not get to those closeups of Baby right away?

The friends you invite in to see your films, however, aren't familiar with that room. If you stick to closeups alone, your audience will be interrupting constantly to ask where various scenes were taken. And you'll have to establish the shots by saying: "Oh, that was taken in the bedroom . . . That was taken in the living room . . . That's in the upstairs hall. . . ."

In addition, closeups in themselves will not do Baby justice. Of course you want to show off the baby's best points, but if you throw closeups at your audience before building up with establishing and medium shots, Uncle Hal and Neighbor Montgomery are going to get bored very quickly.

All the above arguments are so many unconvincing words when spoken to a photographer who isn't interested in showing his pictures to someone else. But there's a niche in the Smithsonian Institution for that *rara avis*. It's still empty.

NOT BY THE NUMBERS

Granted, you may say, that the basic elements of the sequence are simple, fundamental, and necessary, nevertheless isn't this one-two-three routine of LS, MS, and CU too rigid, stiff, too much—as the army drill term puts it—"by the numbers"?

It's a pertinent question. But that one-two-three pattern isn't inflexible. There can be lots of leeway in applying it, lots of room for imagination. The last thing in the world we want you to do is to shoot as a matter of mechanical routine. But you did have to learn to crawl before you walked, and you've got to learn your long shot, medium shot, and closeup procedure before going on into more complex phases of continuity.

Thus, as you read on, you will discover how to get all the flexibility you want into the simple sequence, through what you will learn about the varied technique of shooting and, ultimately, through what you will find out about cutting and editing—that final assembling of your film, after it comes back developed and printed, in the exact length and order you desire.

We have been arbitrary in deciding on the order in which we will discuss the various phases of pictorial continuity, and we have had to be. For one authority will argue that study of the general rule should precede overlap, the next will state the reverse, and a third will firmly declare that understanding of cut-ins and cutaways should come before either. It is impossible to agree on the relative importance of these various subjects. All aspects of pictorial continuity are so closely interrelated that we must study the thing whole. For our purpose here we have placed the chapters in an order of precedence which we are certain will present the study of pictorial continuity in a logical manner, and will, at the end of this book, have made a complete picture of it.

SUMMARY

——A motion picture, to be more than just a series of animated snapshots, must have pictorial continuity.

——Pictorial continuity is the proper development and connection of motion-picture sequences to create a smoothly flowing, coherent motion-picture story.

——The sequence is a fundamental unit of continuity and has three basic, all-important elements: long shot, medium shot, and closeup. These elements correspond to the three stages in which the human eye unconsciously views action.

——To avoid the "animated snapshot" type of movie, the cameraman should have his subjects *do* something instead of posing in stilted fashion. He must aim for action. And by applying the technique of pictorial continuity, he can get action into scenes that have no live actors.

——The cameraman must never forget he is shooting for an audience which will view the action secondhand. By being at all times aware of the screen's limitations, he can make the audience see his action on the screen as he saw it in real life.

——The reader will find the apparent one-two-three routine of the LS, MS, and CU is not inflexible. There is lots of leeway in continuity for the photographer's imagination, as will be explained in the chapters to come.

Chapter Two

THE SIMPLE SEQUENCE: VARIATIONS

RELATIVITY

Having looked at the sequence in its simple, most rudimentary form, we turn now to the problem of adding variety and interest. The long shot, the medium shot, and the closeup are all *relative*. Translated, this means that the distances which separate the long shot from the medium and the medium shot from the closeup in an interior sequence such as visiting Mr. Prospect, would be different from the distances involved outdoors in photographing a parade where the LS from the rooftop might be hundreds of feet distant, the MS of the marching ranks from the sidewalk might be fifty feet away, and the final CU as much as twenty feet removed.

Long distances between shots do not necessarily typify outdoor sequences. The distances involved in shooting a parade do not apply in shooting an outdoor sequence of the neighbors' kids playing hopscotch on the sidewalk.

Nor are all indoor sequences restricted in distances between shots. The LS, MS, and CU are vastly different between filming a graduation exercise in a school auditorium and doing a sequence of Junior building a model airplane in the playroom.

An indoor sequence like the graduation exercise, moreover, would call for greater distances between shots than an outdoor sequence showing Mother rocking Baby to sleep in the garden.

Relativity applies as truly to the simple, solid facts of photography as it does to the abstruse world of mathematical physics. The point to remember and the crux of the whole matter is that relativity depends strictly on the personal preference of the cameraman and what he wants to emphasize in his movie.

Two camera fiends—Roscoe and Ross—set out to shoot the same sequence, the heart-warming one of looking over a new car. Roscoe takes his LS from outside the dealer's display lot, showing the dealer's sign and numerous cars. Next, he moves onto the lot for an MS in which one particular car—a dream sedan beside which stands a pretty girl—dominates the screen, although there are parts of other cars showing and the locale is still identified as a dealer's lot. In his CU, the sedan dominates the screen completely. Roscoe feels he has achieved his objective, that of showing the car he intends to buy.

Ross feels differently. To him, what makes the sedan most attractive is its handsomely designed front.

Above—Roscoe's Sequence
  Long Shot
  Medium Shot
  Closeup

Right—Ross' Sequence
  Long Shot
  Medium Shot
  Closeup

He is going to feature that. Ross ignores Roscoe's long shot. "I'm not shooting film to give the auto dealer publicity," he mutters. Instead, he shoots *his* LS from where Roscoe took his medium shot, and this—as we have seen—suffices to establish the locale. He takes *his* MS from where Roscoe took his closeup, and for *his* CU, moves in and fills his viewfinder (and the audience's screen) with the front of the car.

Roscoe and Ross have shot relatively different sequences, both perfectly acceptable. Good continuity was applied in each case, even though the stories differed in emphasis.

(Every knowing cameraman, by the way, will use an actor (a pretty one is always desirable!) to give life and appeal to a scene even though the actor is not the true subject of the movie. Furthermore, the model in the case just given, by appropriate gestures, can draw the eye to the front of the car, the point of interest Ross wishes to indicate to his audience.)

THE EXTREME LONG SHOT

Thus the simple sequence develops and its basic elements reveal themselves to be flexible and elastic. The elasticity can be considerable. The long shot, for instance, can become very long, producing the *extreme long shot* or "ELS," which gives *a far distant view of the area in which action takes place.*

A true ELS of a parade would be taken from an airplane flying overhead. An ELS taken on the ground would be so far removed from a subject—such as a piece of statuary in a park—that the latter would be just barely recognizable for what it was, with plenty of surroundings—a lake, trees, people sitting in the sun—to give a good idea of the locale.

The extreme long shot is also known as a *location shot.* It is so far away that it does not matter if there is action going on or not, because it is too remote to pick up specific details.

THE EXTREME CLOSEUP

Equally, the closeup can contract to the *extreme closeup.* The "ECU," sometimes called an *insert,* is a *closeup of a small detail.*

Suppose you shoot a sequence of Dad giving Mother a ring for her birthday. You have moved in with long and medium shots to a closeup of happy Mom wearing a very handsome ring. Your audience—especially the women in it—would like a closer look at the gift. So Mother holds out her hand and you bring the camera very close for your ECU. When projected, this shot shows the audience part of Mother's hand and the ring in all its sparkling detail looming big on the screen. The diamond is now the size of a man's head, and Dad has really outdone himself!

Relativity of subject matter applies to the insert, too. If you are photographing a locomotive in a station, a shot of one of the huge wheels becomes as much of an ECU as Mother's ring.

THE FULL-FIGURE SHOT

What of the medium shot? It cannot go to any extreme in the direction of long shot or closeup without falling into the category of one or the other. Compared to them, it is pretty limited in range. Very often it takes the form of the most limiting of all motion-picture shots, the *full-figure shot*. The full-figure shot is self-explanatory, and needs no definition. It is relative. It may be made of an adult or child, elephant or dog, a tennis player or an inanimate object like Grant's Tomb.

The full-figure shot usually has a little head- and foot-room to show a trace of background, whereas in the ordinary MS, the lower portion of the figure is frequently cut off once the LS has established it.

SUMMARY

———The LS, MS, and CU are strictly relative. Distances between them are determined by the nature of action and location, by the cameraman's personal preference, and by what he wants to emphasize to his audience.

———The basic elements are elastic. The long shot may stretch to the extreme long shot, or location shot; the closeup may contract to the extreme closeup, or insert. The medium shot, however, has little range and becomes very sharply limited in the full-figure shot.

CHAPTER THREE

THE REESTABLISHING SHOT

CONNECTING SEQUENCES

We have observed that a single sequence such as the sales call on Mr. Prospect will give you a "motion picture" as long as you apply the basic elements of continuity to it. But most of the movies you shoot will be too rich in action to be told in just one sequence. Suppose Mr. Prospect's secretary came to his desk, thereby introducing something new into the scene. Remember that as you finished your simple sequence of Mr. Prospect, you were taking the closeup. Your audience would be unable to see Miss Secretary unless you—the cameraman—enabled it to. Thus you must have another sequence to introduce her and to tell her part in the story. Still more sequences will follow, as new actors and new action are added to the story.

Almost all action breaks down into a series of related sequences. They may be considered as the links of a chain. The links, to make a chain, must be joined; the sequences, to form a coherent motion-picture story, must be tied together. Coherence is obtained through good continuity, and for good continuity properly tied motion-picture sequences are indispensable.

The photographic device that joins sequences together is called a *reestablishing shot,* or "RS." It is a medium or long shot that gets its name from the fact that it usually follows a closeup and *again establishes the general scene,* much as the original LS established it in the beginning.

So, in the case in point, you *pull back* far enough with your camera in order that your next shot may show the general scene again, with Miss Secretary actually entering it. Your audience is instantly oriented with regard to the appearance of Miss Secretary; it understands that she *came from somewhere* beyond the screen boundary and did not magically appear from the floor beside Mr. Prospect. And you can go ahead and shoot your second sequence, involving Miss Secretary.

Bear in mind that the prime purpose of reestablishing the old scene is to carry action smoothly into a new sequence. Such action may take place either in the old physical setting or in a new one. Your second sequence began with a reestablishing shot showing Miss Secretary entering the office and then going through the action of taking dictation from Mr. Prospect. Your third sequence could take place in her own office and show her typing out the dictation. The RS necessary to connect the second and third sequences would show her leaving Mr. Prospect's office to enter her own.

REESTABLISH FOR ANYTHING NEW!

Whenever anything new is introduced on the screen, whether that something new is a live actor or an inanimate object, you should reestablish.

Suppose you shoot a picture of Brother Jonathan working on his radio. This picture calls for a lot of big closeups, because the radio parts are small. First, however, you shoot a regular LS-MS-CU sequence to introduce the workshop, the radio set, and Jonathan.

After your first closeup, you reestablish to show him in a new action—removing a tube from the set. This RS need not take in the whole workshop. It can be just another MS to tie Jonathan in with the radio again.

Since the tube is the cause of the trouble, you favor it with a closeup, and even one or more ECU's as Jonathan examines it. This done, you reestablish with another shot of him replacing the tube and screwing in the backboard.

You can now end your movie with a final shot of Jonathan satisfiedly giving ear to his rejuvenated radio; or you can add as many more sequences as you wish, showing him tinkering with other parts and using different tools, *as long as you reestablish with each new action.*

The frequent use of reestablishing shots is necessary to refresh the audience's memory of the scene, of the relation of the radio to Jonathan, and of the relation of the parts shown in the inserts to the radio as a whole. It is a continuity truism that an audience, always looking ahead to what is coming, *rarely keeps in mind more than one scene prior to the one it is looking at.* It must periodically be reminded of how a small scene fits into the larger scene that includes it.

Remember that the human eye unconsciously refuses to look at too many closeups in succession, and reorients itself every now and then by a quick look around. Let your camera do likewise for your audience by frequently reestablishing the scene, otherwise confusion may kill interest.

You reestablish, therefore, not only to tie sequences together, but also to keep your audience from getting lost.

REESTABLISHING BY PULLING BACK

There are three ways of making a reestablishing shot. We have already used one in our explanation: *pulling back,* the simplest method. The other two are *panning* and the *reverse-angle shot.* All three methods can frequently be applied to the same story. Let us take one example for all three and see how it works out.

Your good friend and neighbor, Mr. Montgomery, is going to provide you with your action. Montgomery, who is a stickler for proper inflation in his automobile tires, is outdoors checking their air pressure with a gauge.

Using what you have learned so far, you make a movie of this action. You take an LS from across the street showing the car parked in front of the house and Neighbor Montgomery standing beside the left rear tire. Your MS follows from a position in the middle of the street and advances the action: it shows Montgomery kneeling to apply the gauge to the tire valve. Finally, in your CU, he is actually applying the gauge to the valve and reading the pressure. (An ECU showing just the gauge and the reading on it would be logical—but optional—at this point.)

You have now completed your first sequence. Next, Mr. Montgomery rises, walks over to the left front tire, and repeats his performance. This separate action constitutes a separate sequence, and therefore you must reestablish in order to tie it to the first sequence.

The first method of reestablishing is to *pull back* to a medium- or long-shot position, whichever is back far enough to include both the rear tire, the location from which Montgomery is *coming,* and the front tire, the location to which he is *going.* Then you move in again for medium and closeup shots of him at the front tire.

REESTABLISHING BY PANNING

The second method of reestablishing is by *panning* (derived from the word "panorama"). After pulling back from the closeup, the camera is panned to *follow* the action as it moves from one location to another.

You would pan Mr. Montgomery by following him through the camera's viewfinder as he moved from the rear to the front tire, carrying your audience along from one point to another.

So much can be said on the subject of the pan that, now we have explained its use as a reestablishing shot, we are going to postpone further discussion until a later

THE REESTABLISHING SHOT

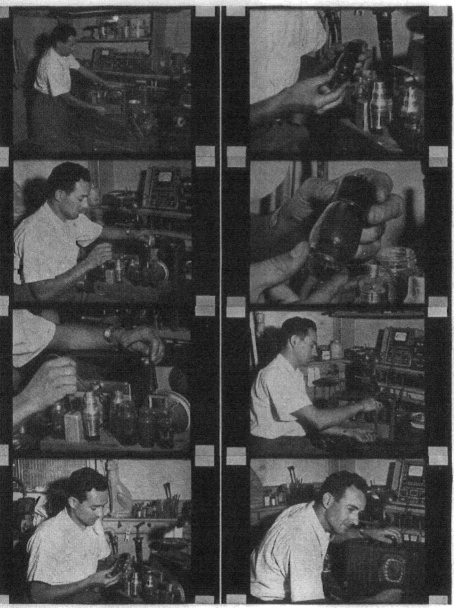

Establishing Shot
Medium Shot
Closeup
Reestablishing Shot

Closeup
Extreme Closeup
Reestablishing Shot
Medium Shot

SIMPLE SEQUENCE

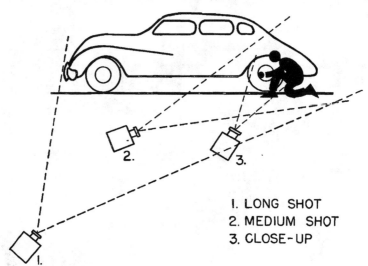

1. LONG SHOT
2. MEDIUM SHOT
3. CLOSE-UP

REESTABLISHING BY PULLING BACK

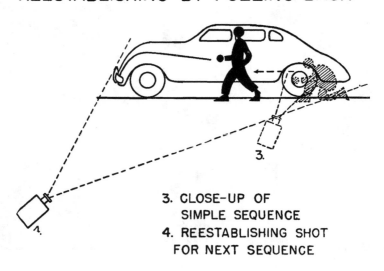

3. CLOSE-UP OF
   SIMPLE SEQUENCE
4. REESTABLISHING SHOT
   FOR NEXT SEQUENCE

REESTABLISHING BY REVERSE ANGLE

3. CLOSE−UP OF SIMPLE SEQUENCE
4. REESTABLISHING SHOT FOR NEXT SEQUENCE
5. REVERSE ANGLE OF 4

REESTABLISHING BY PANNING

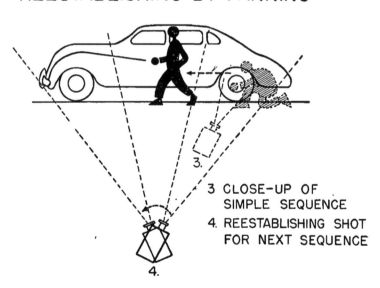

3 CLOSE−UP OF SIMPLE SEQUENCE

4. REESTABLISHING SHOT FOR NEXT SEQUENCE

chapter where we can go more thoroughly into the various aspects of handling this photographic "hot potato."

REESTABLISHING WITH THE REVERSE ANGLE

Now we proceed to the third method of reestablishing—the *reverse-angle shot.*

When we say reverse-angle shot, we mean a shot wherein the camera has been turned around a full 180 degrees and is facing in exactly the opposite direction. It is thus always a two-shot affair, with a preceding shot to give the angle from which the switch to reverse is made.

Here is Mr. Montgomery again to act for your reverse-angle shot. You shoot your first sequence of him checking the rear tire as you did originally. Now, as he rises, you change position by moving to the rear bumper directly behind him and the rear tire, so that you are shooting past him along the car to the front tire.

In the next sequence, you move the camera down past the front tire and shoot *back* toward the rear tire. Now you catch Montgomery moving *away from* the rear tire and *toward* the front tire, and you have a reverse-angle shot.

Varying your reestablishing shots will enrich your sequences and avoid monotony. Be guided by story needs—and by good sense.

SUMMARY

——All action breaks down into motion-picture sequences.

———A new sequence is necessary wherever a new subject, live or inanimate, is introduced into the picture, or when the subject is moved from an old to a new location.

———In order to join motion-picture sequences together, the reestablishing shot is used.

———The RS not only ties sequences together but also keeps the audience from getting confused or lost.

———There are three ways to reestablish: by pulling back, by panning, and by shooting from a reverse angle.

CHAPTER FOUR

OVERLAP AND MATCHING ACTION

CURING JUMPY ACTION

Good continuity demands a smooth, uninterrupted flow of action from one shot to the next. That impression of smoothness is destroyed for the audience when there are sudden gaps in the movement of screen actors between shots.

If (returning to the original example) your first shot of Mr. Prospect shows him starting to rise from his chair, and your next shows him standing erect, the audience may be conscious of an irritating jump in the action, as though the few feet of film showing Mr. Prospect going through the act of rising had been cut out.

This "jumpy action" is hard on the audience's eyes—and harder on your reputation as a cameraman and cutter. A cure is *overlap.* Defining this brand-new term, we say that overlap is *the reshooting of action that has taken place at the tail end of the preceding scene.*

MATCHING ACTION
(Between shots)

Medium Shot

Closeup

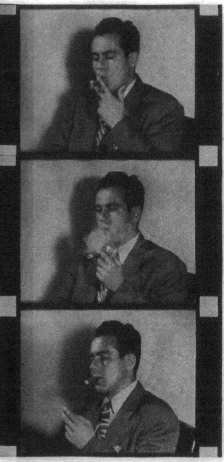

Try shooting a sequence of Cousin Robert relaxing over a good cigar. You start in MS position and take a shot showing him sitting with the lit cigar, admiring the nice long ash, putting the cigar to his lips for a drag, and blowing out the smoke. At this point you stop the camera and move in for a closeup.

But before you start your CU, you ask Cousin Robert to repeat the final action of the medium shot. From CU position, you press the button as he once again raises the cigar for a drag, and exhales. Then you continue on with your closeup and new action.

Stop for a moment and look at what you have done. If you screen the sequence, you will see that you have two shots, from different positions, showing identical action. This is the footage that comprises the overlap. (There would be the same result had you made an LS-to-MS sequence of Cousin Robert.)

Now with your finished movie, as you want the audience to see it, you are obviously not going to show both pieces of action in their entirety. This sort of repetition would be worse from an audience's point of view than a gap in the action. So you avoid it, when editing the film, by performing a film-cutting operation known as *matching action*.

HOW TO MATCH ACTION

To match action in the overlap of Cousin Robert, you pick a frame in your MS footage and a frame in your CU footage where the action is most identical. Take as example the frames where Cousin Robert has placed the cigar in his mouth. You discard everything that comes *after* this frame in the MS, and everything that comes *before* the identical frame in the CU. Then you splice the two shots together.

The frames where Cousin Robert has just put the cigar in his mouth serve your purpose best because it is easiest to match action at a point in the film where the action is comparatively slow or where it has stopped altogether. As you gain experience and deftness in editing, however, you should practice matching action *on motion,* such as the point where Cousin Robert is in the act of removing the cigar from his mouth and blowing out the smoke. A much smoother transition between scenes results, inasmuch as the audience's eye is busy following movement, instead of pausing at a static point in the action.

The human eye watching Cousin Robert does not need overlap because, unlike the camera which stops shooting when you change distance or angle, it does not stop looking at Cousin Robert even while it moves around the room. By using overlap, the eyes of your audience may also look at him without being made conscious of interruptions while positions are being changed.

CONTROLLED AND UNCONTROLLED ACTION

You can readily see that for a cameraman to shoot overlap, he must be able to *control* the action so that his subject will repeat it at the beginning of the next shot.

The home cameraman will be able to control action quite often because his subjects will be intimate ones, such as the family at home eating Sunday dinner, or vacation friends on the beach.

If the action cannot be controlled—if your subject is Baby romping in her playpen, or a four-alarm fire, or a professional tennis match—overlap can still be made by using two or more cameras instead of just one.

This, of course, calls for one or two confederates with additional cameras—ideally three—stationed at LS, MS, and CU positions. To get the overlap, you simply start your MS camera rolling just before you stop your LS, and start the CU before ending your MS shot.

If you have only two cameras, the best solution is to assign one to take both the LS and MS shots, and the other to do just the CU work. Overlap then occurs only on the MS and CU shots, but this is the most efficient compromise, since once your scene has been established you are bound to use more MS than LS shots.

Once in a lifetime you will have a story where instead of shooting regular overlap, you will want to run three cameras simultaneously throughout the entire length of a movie sequence, so that the complete action will be registered on three separate strips of film, each taken from a different position: one, entirely a long shot; another, a medium shot; and the third, a closeup. You will then be able, when editing, to cut back and forth between LS, MS, and CU *anywhere* in the film, matching action between every shot. The possibilities for constant variety are self-evident.

This procedure naturally involves a great deal of

expense in film expenditure and a great deal of difficulty in assembling a camera team from among your photographer friends. It would be too much to undertake such a project unless you had an opportunity to shoot an exceedingly rare or important story that would never be repeated—the President of the United States dedicating a local hospital, or engineers dynamiting the side of a mountain to make way for a new road.

This expensive procedure is followed in the professional film world when shooting unusual newsreel subjects, such as a championship boxing match, or during movie-making when the shot involves the destruction of a costly set. Never-to-be-repeated scenes virtually demand several cameras running simultaneously from different positions and angles to assure complete coverage.

WHEN CONTROLLED ACTION IS IMPOSSIBLE

Although overlap should usually be considered a "must" by the cameraman, occasions will arise when it will be impossible to match action between shots.

What happens, for instance, when you have uncontrolled action such as Baby romping in her playpen, and you cannot get another cameraman to shoot overlap for you? Well, you don't abandon that appealing subject just because you can't match action between shots! Of course not. You shoot Baby just the same and resign yourself to a slight jump between shots.

But you can minimize that jump between shots by taking pains to pick up your subject in approximately the same position and action as at the tail end of your last shot. This can usually be done with home subjects. If your LS of Baby ended with her in the center of the playpen, catch her in the center again when you begin your MS. If her action at the end of the LS was to put a rattle in her mouth—an action she is extremely likely to repeat—start your MS as she does it again. While it isn't likely that the movements will be so closely similar that you'll be enabled to match action, the similarity that does exist will help a lot to smooth over the jump between shots.

There will even be certain times when overlap can be entirely dispensed with, because the audience will not notice the failure to match action. Take that subject mentioned earlier—vacation friends on the beach. If your scene is a general one showing many people doing various things—swimming, throwing a medicine ball around—which are all going on at the same time, it isn't necessary to match action from LS to MS as you move your camera closer to the scene. Your audience still sees a variety of actions, and since it is not following one action specifically, it will not be conscious of slight jumps between shots. If you move in on one specific action, however, and oblige your audience to follow it to the exclusion of any other, then you must overlap if possible.

The professional cutter talks of shots which move smoothly from one to the next as shots which "cut together." Overlap is essential for scenes to cut together well. Since you will probably do most of your own cutting, overlap whenever you can.

SUMMARY

——Jumpy action destroys that impression of smoothness between shots in a sequence which is a mark of good continuity.

——Overlap is a cure for jumpy action. It is the reshooting of action that has taken place at the tail end of the previous scene.

——Overlap makes possible the matching of action between successive shots by picking frames in each where the action is identical, regardless of a difference in angle or distance from the subject.

——Overlap can be made by the individual cameraman when the action is controlled. When the action is uncontrolled, overlap is possible through the use of additional cameras.

——In the case of never-to-be-repeated scenes, it pays to run several cameras simultaneously from various positions throughout the entire action, so that the editor can cut between LS, MS, and CU anywhere in the film.

——When it is impossible to get overlap, new shots should be begun with the subject's position and action as similar as possible to what they were at the end of the preceding shot.

——Occasionally overlap can be dispensed with when shooting a general scene with various activities going on, since the audience will be too busy trying to follow the several activities at once to notice the failure to match action between shots.

CHAPTER FIVE

CUT-INS AND CUT-AWAYS

INCIDENTAL SHOTS

We are making good headway in our study of continuity. We have taken note of the structure of the sequence, of how sequences are connected, and of how those connections are made smoother and more interesting to an audience. So far we have an outline, a skeleton form of continuity.

We now take a look at certain shots which will serve to develop that outline, add substance to that skeleton.

These are shots which are *in addition to* the LS, MS, and CU which carry the main action of the sequence. Such incidental shots are known as *cut-ins* and *cut-aways*, or simply *cuts*. They are brief shots, and are usually closeups and extreme closeups, or occasionally medium shots.

Cut-ins and cut-aways are among the most versatile devices in continuity, useful in many ways, rich in material. They are secondary but indispensable, as vital to the proper operation of a movie as ball bearings are to the motor of an automobile.

THE CUT-IN

The cut-in derives its name from the fact that it *cuts into the main action.* In a sequence showing two friends meeting, a CU of their handshake is a cut-in. If your subject is packing for a vacation, and you wish to show how well traveled his bags are, your ECU of the hotel labels constitutes a cut-in. You are using cut-ins when, in a sequence of Johnny taking the dog for a walk, you take an ECU of his hand snapping the leash onto the dog collar, or a CU of the dog's legs as it trots off.

THE CUT-AWAY

Brother shot of the cut-in, equally valuable although using categorically opposite subject matter, is the cut-away. Although it, too, can be a CU, ECU, or MS, it does not cut *into* the main action, but *cuts away to a related subject or to a separate action that is going on at the same time.*

The movie sequences with which we illustrated the cut-in also serve to provide examples of the cut-away. In the sequence of two friends meeting, a cut-away would be a CU of the smiling face of a third friend watching the other two. In the vacation sequence, a cut-away would move the camera from the main action of frantic packing to the anxious face of a friend urging haste, or to a taxi driver outside waiting impatiently for the vacationers to appear. In the case of Johnny walking the dog, a shot of Mother, or Johnny's

Top to Bottom

Establishing Shot
Medium Shot
Closeup

Cut-in
Cut-away
Reestablishing Shot

VARIATIONS OF THE CUT-IN

Above—Head-on Shot

Below—Tail-away Shot

pal Freddy watching him put the leash on the dog, would be a cut-away.

A thought to bear in mind regarding the cut-away is that it should always be *established in relation to the main action.*

In our last illustration we suggested a shot of Mother or of Freddy as a cut-away. It is important that Mother or Freddy should have been seen in an earlier shot, in an LS, for example. Even though they may be merely background figures in that shot, their presence has been established, and there is no surprise or confusion to the audience when they suddenly appear on-screen in a cut-away.

(It is not necessary to establish cut-ins, on the other hand, because a cut-in is part of the main action and is therefore automatically established in one of the main shots of the sequence.)

The practice of establishing cuts has its exceptions, like so many other practices of good continuity. It is sometimes ignored in highly specialized movie forms like newsreels or documentaries. These forms are extremely economical of footage and depend strongly on *narration* to tie shots together.

For example, an audience may see an MS or CU of the President seated in the White House announcing the opening of a great new dam in the West, and this shot will be followed by an extreme long shot of the dam as it goes into operation. The lack of good continuity technique would make the succession of shots confusing or meaningless without the aid of the "crutch" of narration.

HEAD-ONS AND TAIL-AWAYS

Cut-ins of action may take the form of *head-on* or *tail-away* shots.

The head-on is simply a shot of the action *directly approaching* the camera. It is coming "head-on" or "full-face." Johnny and his friend walking directly toward the camera would be a head-on. This type of shot is often used as a genuine LS in order to introduce a sequence.

The directness of the head-on can give it a strong dramatic quality. One of the punchiest shots in photography is the repeatedly used head-on approach of an auto, tank, horses, or marching men, shot from ground level, and showing the moving subject passing directly overhead.

The *tail-away* is the exact opposite of the head-on shot, and depicts action from the rear as it moves *away* from the camera. If you shoot the action of Johnny walking down the street with his friend and the dog from the rear, with the subjects moving away from the camera, you have a tail-away.

This shot has novelty and drama and is popular for ending a sequence. The movement of a subject away from the camera, and the diminution in size as it recedes, strongly suggest that the action in that sequence is completed, whether it be a shot of a cowboy galloping off toward the horizon in a "Western," or your own picture of Uncle Hal walking down the street toward the railroad station after paying you a visit.

WIDER USES

We are limiting this chapter on cut-ins and cut-aways. It is little more than an introduction to these extremely useful and important shots. We wish here only to define and describe them. We will have more to say about them very soon, notably in the chapters on directional continuity and buildup, and we will show to what varied uses they lend themselves.

SUMMARY

——Cut-ins and cut-aways are among the most useful devices in pictorial continuity. They are incidental shots, additional to the main action. They are usually CU's and ECU's and sometimes MS's.

——The cut-in gets its name from the fact that it cuts into the main action, whereas the cut-away does exactly the opposite and cuts away to a related subject or to a separate action that is going on at the same time.

——Care should be taken to have the cut-away subject established in the main action before the actual cut-away is used.

——Head-on and tail-away shots are specialized types of cut-in. The head-on is a shot of action as it directly approaches the camera, while the tail-away, its opposite, depicts the action from the rear as it moves away from the camera.

——Cut-ins and cut-aways have important and varied uses which will be discussed in future chapters.

CHAPTER SIX

THE GENERAL RULE

A REAL "MUST"

So vital to smooth continuity is the avoidance or minimizing of jumpy action that we are going to do something we haven't done before—lay down a hard-and-fast rule which *must* be followed.

We call it *the general rule,* because it is applied to all the shots of a motion-picture sequence, without exception, consistently, *generally.*

The general rule states: *When shooting a new scene, change the size of the image, or change the angle, or both.*

We dislike the word "must"; the technique of pictorial continuity is so highly flexible, so much depends on the imaginative spark of the individual photographer, that we prefer to use the word "should" even when we strongly feel something ought to be done. But there is no such qualification as "should" for the general rule. As its name unmistakably implies, it is used everywhere; it must be and can be.

It can be done by you as cameraman while shooting a sequence, or by you as cutter when editing the film (by using cut-ins and cut-aways—but remember that you, as the cutter, cannot put into the film something you as the cameraman left out when the picture was shot, so shoot those extra cuts!)

Why all the fuss about a change of image size or of angle with every new shot? The reasons are two: the first is the fact that this simple operation always makes it possible to cover up any jump in the action because the audience's attention will be taken up by the "something different, something new" created by the change; and the second reason is variety, to achieve which the general rule is the basic, unfailing means.

OUTWITTING JUMPY ACTION FROM THE FLANK

All this to-do about the general rule's covering up jumpy action will not, we hope, cause you to hesitate about applying it. Truth is, you have been using it from the very beginning; you have been changing the size of the image every time you moved from long shot to medium shot, from medium shot to closeup. You did it in the sequence on Cousin Robert in the study of overlap.

Overlap eliminates jumpy action by overpowering it with a frontal attack, so to speak. The general rule outwits it by a deceptive play around the flanks. The best solution is a "combined operation" where both overlap and the general rule can be employed, such as in the sequence of Cousin Robert smoking his cigar. But let us take a case where overlap is impossible—

where the action cannot be controlled and where there is only one camera at work—to see how the general rule can be most useful and most necessary.

You have certainly seen the work of a cameraman who starts to shoot a scene, stops the camera in order to save film until something more interesting develops, then starts shooting again without changing position or lens. The result is an inevitable jump between shots which is hard on the audience eye and classifies the cameraman immediately as an awkward novice.

Take, for example, that frequently photographed sequence of a child climbing the steps of a slide. Proud Dad began to shoot when little sister Betty was clambering up the first few steps; as she moved slowly from step to step, Dad began to wonder whether his film would last until she got to the top, so he stopped the camera when Betty was about halfway up. Then, as she got to the final step, he started his camera again *without changing position* and caught her as she triumphantly scrambled over onto the top of the slide.

On-screen, to all appearances, Betty has literally jumped from the middle steps to the top rung. It is a remarkable performance, but rather disturbing to the audience even though the sequence be entitled "Child of Superman."

Now you shoot the sequence the right way, by applying the general rule. You'll find that you can be just as economical with Dad's film. Here's how you'd do it.

You start with Betty on the first steps, and you stop your camera as before, when she has reached the halfway mark. But instead of staying in the same position for your next shot, you move in for an MS—make it a full-figuré—as she continues her climb. Finally, a closeup catches Betty's gleeful expression as she comes up the last step. You can reestablish as Betty pulls herself onto the slide itself.

In this example you change the image size by *enlarging* it when you move the camera closer to the subject with the MS and the CU. In the RS you would change the image size by pulling back and *decreasing* it.

You can see how a change of image size creates a *different* scene, gives you something right at the beginning to attract the audience's attention so that it will overlook a jump in the action. Although it is aware that Betty has traveled some distance between the original LS and the RS, its eye has not been irritated, nor has its sense of logic been disturbed. The new approach the camera has taken toward its subject by a change of image size stimulates the audience, whose imagination cheerfully carries it through the unimportant action the camera has chosen to ignore.

The "something different" provided by the general rule, that *variety* which gives novelty to each shot and stimulates audience interest afresh, is a quality some cameramen consider even more important than the fact that the rule can cover up a jump in the action.

They contend that variety soothes the audience's eye, which is bound to tire if it looks at the same scene too long. Equally important, they believe the constant change to something different and interesting gives the motion picture a snap and movement it must have to be really good.

At any rate you, regardless of which you consider the more important, have *two excellent* reasons why you must use the general rule.

ANGLES

Changing the image size is one way of putting the general rule into operation. A change of angle can smooth over a jump in the action or provide variety just as effectively, at times even better.

Angles provide infinite opportunities for attaining that "something different," opportunities which can be tremendously exciting and dramatic. Consider just one minor example—Betty making that epic stair climb. Instead of just changing your image size, you change angles with every shot in the sequence. Your LS again is the same, but the MS is taken from the side looking up, and the CU is slightly off from a ninety-degree angle at eye level, while your final RS is a reverse angle. There is no question but that you have greatly increased the interest and animation of the sequence.

There is no need to make a choice between changing image size and changing the angle when shooting a new scene. There is no conflict, for the two work hand in hand and one improves the other. The two should be used together whenever possible. Remember the words of the general rule: When shooting a new scene, change the size of the image, or change the angle, *or both*.

LENS CHANGES

So far you have changed the image size only by moving toward or away from your subject. But you can also change image size back and forth, make it larger or smaller, *without moving your camera*—by putting on a lens of a different focal length.

. Such lenses are either *long* (telephoto) or *wide-angle:* the former enlarges the image size, the latter decreases it. The regular 16-mm. camera (so called because it uses 16 mm. width film) takes a 25-mm. or one-inch lens for its standard image size. A long lens of 50 mm. brings the camera halfway to the subject (doubling the size of the image) , while a four-inch lens brings it four times as close.

A wide-angle lens, which is 15 mm. for the regular 16-mm. camera, reduces the size of the image by almost half.

The 8-mm. and 35-mm. cameras have similar lenses producing similar effects.

Although long lenses and wide-angle lenses are supplementary and not part of the standard equipment of most non-professionals (and indeed, there are few pictures which cannot be shot without them) , their occasional usefulness in the operation of the general rule makes them worth a note on proper handling. The chief caution to bear in mind is their unusual effect on perspective.

A long lens, for instance, pulls the background unnaturally close to the subject, flattens the perspective, and requires you to be very careful of focus. When two or more subjects are in line, a long lens foreshortens the distance between the nearer and farther objects, as you will see very clearly if you use a long lens in a shot from behind home plate taking in both the pitcher and the batter in a baseball game. When the pitcher hurls the ball, his outflung arm seems to come within inches of the batter's face. Such a shot is essentially a stunt, and does nothing in itself to further the aim of good continuity.

Still, there are times when a telephoto lens is a great help. It can be a real boon when you are faced with the problem of shooting objects at tremendous distances, such as a majestic mountain peak from across a valley. The standard lens will give you an extreme long shot while the long lens will enable you to come closer without moving.

Employing a long lens is just about unavoidable when photographing action from a position where movement back and forth is difficult, such as shooting a football game from the stands, or in cases where the action moves too quickly—as in a horse race—to give you time to change position from LS to MS. But here again you must be careful about the use of the long lens. A head-on CU of horses taken with a long lens gives them the appearance of just bobbing up and down—not running ahead at all!

Their greater power of magnification makes telephoto lenses excellent for inserts, especially if close approach to the subject is impossible, as is often the case in zoos, museums, or exhibit halls. And even when a subject is accessible, it may be possible to get the picture only if one keeps one's distance and uses a long lens. When photographing wild life a close approach might scare the subject away, and this applies equally to human beings—whether children or politicians—

whose awareness of the photographer often makes them freeze in self-consciousness or else "mug" the camera to the ruination of a natural picture.

Sometimes the matter of accessibility works in reverse. Instead of being too far away, you find yourself too close for a standard lens to take in all you want to photograph. Physical limitations within doors, or outdoors on a narrow street, may make it impossible for you to back off far enough to get everything in. The solution to this problem is the wide-angle lens, which gives your camera a much greater *breadth of vision*. It will also give you even more extreme closeups than a long lens.

As a last word on special lenses for continuity purposes, we want to say again that *there are few pictures indeed that cannot be shot without them*. These lenses are strictly *accessory*, and do not replace the standard lens any more than binoculars replace the human eye. Don't use them to excess; don't go "lens-happy."

SUMMARY

——The one rule of pictorial continuity that can and *must* invariably be used is the so-called general rule, which states: When shooting a new scene, change the size of the image, or change the angle, or both.

——Image size can be changed by moving closer to or farther away from the subject, and this is accomplished through the LS, MS, CU, and the reestablishing shot.

——The general rule covers up jumpy action by distracting the audience's attention through the addition

of something different to the new scene, and also en-
riches the motion picture by injecting variety.

——Angle changes provide infinite ways of applying
the general rule.

——Image size can also be changed by use of supplementary lenses such as long lenses, which enlarge the
image size, or wide-angle lenses, which decrease it while
enlarging the angle of vision.

——Supplementary lenses can be very convenient at
times, but the photographer should never forget they
can only supplement—not replace—the functions of
the standard lens.

THE GENERAL RULE

No change of Image Size
or Angle
(All action contained in
one long shot)

THE GENERAL RULE

Change of Image Size only

Long Shot
Medium Shot
Closeup

THE GENERAL RULE
(Change of Image Size and Angle)

Establishing Shot

Medium Shot

Closeup

Reestablishing Shot

Oblique Angle

Flat Angles

ANGLES

High Angle

Low Angle

CHAPTER SEVEN

ANGLES

CHOICE OF ANGLES

The general rule approves of a change of angles with each new scene. Such a change assures smooth continuity and variety. But just how good, how effective that change will be, is up to the photographer.

Angles are a main ingredient of the cameraman's style. His choice of angles is as fundamental and important in his work as an author's choice of words. Angles can create drama, excitement, suspense. A story can be told more concisely in one good angle shot than in several scenes whose angles are uninspired.

Some of Hollywood's most brilliant cinematographers have made their reputations through a resourceful use of angles. They have rejuvenated subjects that were shot a thousand times before, removing all triteness with one dramatic, unexpected angle.

The usual angle of vision is the straight, normal, eye-level angle. As the eye moves along in its daily operations, this angle is constantly, infinitely varied by high

angles looking down on some subject, low angles looking up, and side angles. There is an endless shifting
and combination of these angles as we walk down the
street, buy a paper, board a bus, gaze up at our office
building as we enter, glance down at our desk to see
what mail has come. And as with the human eye, there
are endless variations for the resourceful camera.

THE FLAT ANGLE

There is one type of angle, however, which is more
a hindrance than a help. It is the so-called *flat angle*.
Despite its name, it is really no angle at all. It is a
direct head-on view, with the plane of the camera
exactly parallel to the plane of the subject. So observed, the subject cannot be seen "in the round," lacks
depth, becomes flat and two-dimensional.

Look through your viewfinder at the side or the front
of a car from a flat angle. Then try an oblique angle off
to one side, so that your viewfinder takes in the front of
the car as well as the side; immediately the subject
gains depth and variety.

The flat angle is particularly to be guarded against
in *stationary* subjects like a house or a motionless person. However, it becomes a useful tool when shooting
subjects moving toward the camera head-on—such sequences as a child running right at you, which carries
constant interest because of the motion. Although the
shot is flat, the angle of vision is constantly changing,
and change makes for variety.

THE POWER OF ANGLES

Camera angles can control an audience's attention and reactions to a remarkable degree. They can emphasize *what* you want your audience to see and *how* you want them to see it.

Shrewd "angling" of the camera will enable you to control background and foreground and eliminate any feature that distracts from the subject.

High angles (in which the camera looks down) ordinarily give the illusion of reducing the height of a subject and slowing down its motion; *low angles* (in which the camera looks up) exaggerate height, and speed up subject motion when comparatively near the camera.

Try shooting Junior from an upper story window of the house as he rides his tricycle on the sidewalk. Then hop downstairs and drop to one knee with your camera as he passes by. You will soon see how angles have affected your subject's size and speed of movement. For one thing, your high angle creates a certain feeling of "superiority" in the audience. It looks *down* on Junior. His size is foreshortened, he appears earthbound, his action seems insignificant. But when the next shot shows Junior from a low angle looking *up,* audience psychology is reversed. Junior gains stature; he commands attention; there is drama and excitement in his actions.

Side angles are valuable for giving depth and perspective to people or objects. They help the audience see the subject in the round. Cleverly used, side angles can make a subject appear thinner or chubbier, as the cameraman desires.

While head-on angles give the illusion of reducing speed, side angles—especially the right angle—appear to increase speed. Suppose you shoot a sequence of the last lap of a horse race from a position at the finish line. If you make a long shot as the leading horses start down the home stretch, your head-on angle will make their movements seem slow compared to the flashing speed of a right-angle shot as they dart past your camera at the finish line.

But don't bet any money on a horse shot from a low side angle. That exaggerated speed is just a powerful illusion.

ANGLES AND PSYCHOLOGY

More is involved in the use of angles than merely the audience's concepts of movement and distance. We have noted how a high or low angle changes audience psychology. A definite emotional and mental attitude can be invoked by taking advantage of the audience's instinctive urge to identify itself with the camera viewpoint.

Suppose you are shooting sequences of Mother with her child in a carriage. If your shots in the first sequence are from a normal eye-level angle, the audience is inclined to feel that it is a bystander, a spectator.

But if, in your next sequence, you shoot Baby using a high angle from the spot where Mother is standing—from Mother's viewpoint, as it were—the audience will unconsciously identify itself with her. And if you take a third sequence shooting Mother from Baby's position in the carriage, with a low angle, your audience will associate itself with Baby, and look at things from her point of view.

DON'T BE "ANGLE CRAZY"!

So stimulating and rewarding are angle shots that the cameraman may be tempted to let his enthusiasm gallop away with his judgment. Being "angle crazy" is as bad as being "pan happy." Angles, like any other aspect of motion-picture technique, are only a means to an end—the objective of good continuity. If they are indulged in for their own sake, they become trick shots, nothing more.

Trick angles might be justified if you were shooting a circus movie, where the freak, the grotesque, and the exaggerated are the order of the day. But the everyday world is not a circus world, and ordinary happenings are not usually observed from bizarre angles.

An angle so unusual that the audience's concentration is interrupted by the thought: "My, what an amazing shot!" is a poor one because you have interfered with your audience's attention to the main action.

On the other hand, if an unusual angle points up the action and strengthens the audience's concentration, it is a good angle, for then the audience is *not* conscious of the angle *as such* and its attention is not distracted from the action.

Suppose two men are sitting at a table playing cards. A low-angle shot of the host, taken from the level of his calf looking up at him, would be an unusual angle all right, but nothing would be gained by it except the impression that the cameraman had tried something in the way of a trick. The main action still is *the card-playing*.

If the host's dog comes along, however, and rubs against his leg, disturbing him, a low-angle shot from the dog's level would be ideal to tell the story of how the host is distracted and looks down at the animal. The main action is now provided *by the dog* and the low angle now becomes the most effective one. It contributes to, it improves the action; it is an integral part of the picture.

Smoothness, may we say again, is one of the outstanding qualities of good continuity. A smooth movie style must avoid angles that irritate and call attention to themselves, just as a smooth writing style must avoid similes or metaphors that are pretentious or too odd.

A good angle, in short, is one that calls attention to the action—not to itself.

SUMMARY

———A cameraman's choice of angles is a main ingredient of his style.

———A change of angles between shots not only enables application of the general rule; it also brings drama and excitement to the action.

———The human eye-level angle is constantly varied by high, low, and side angles.

———The so-called "flat angle" lacks interest and should be avoided except when the subject is moving head-on toward the camera, in which case the motion itself creates the interest.

———Angles can mold an audience's concept of the size and speed of movement of the subject on-screen. They can also influence the audience's psychological attitude toward the subject.

———Don't be "angle crazy." Avoid excessive use of unusual angles, which contribute to a picture only if they serve to clarify it and further the action.

———A good angle is one that calls attention to the action, not to itself.

CHAPTER EIGHT

PANNING

CAUTION! PANNING AHEAD!

We come now to the subject of *panning,* which we have previously (in connection with its usefulness in the reestablishing shot) mentioned as a photographic "hot potato." We approach it in a hesitant, reluctant manner because, like the fabled jewel of India whose curse brought both pleasure and pain to its possessor, the pan can both enrich a movie and create a lot of grief for the unwary cameraman.

Indiscriminate panning is the most common fault of the non-professional photographer. It arises from the utterly mistaken fancy that a motion picture is most truly *moving* when the camera itself is in motion; that if the ball in a tennis game is jumping back and forth across the net, the camera must jump too.

This fallacy has caused many horrible mistakes to be committed in the name of panning. Audiences pay for them in eyesore and irritation. You may have a fine time making your pan, but if it bothers your audience, your reputation as a cameraman is worth less than a piece of light-struck film.

Like drinking for some people, panning is best when done least. However, a pan does have its uses in providing variety and excitement, and there are certain times when it is just about compulsory. That phrase "certain times" is most important. You must learn the right occasion for the pan—and the right way of doing it. So, if you must gratify that overpowering temptation to pan, hold back until you learn the principles of *when* and *how*.

THE "WHEN" OF PANNING

Panning is rightly used *to follow action*. It is a natural type of shot for filming a horse race or catching Junior as he pedals down the sidewalk on his tricycle. These sequences could be covered—in most cases—by pulling back to a long shot instead of by panning. But the shots—especially that of the galloping ponies— would be less effective on-screen. Following action is the most justifiable excuse for panning.

In photographing a *static scene,* where there is no movement in or out of the frame, panning is *only rarely* justified. There are certain specialized cases. Scenic panning, for instance, can be excused when the subject is of such epic dimensions—New York harbor or the Grand Canyon—that only the full sweep of the pan can do it justice.

Panning would be appropriate to show the intricate industrial relationship of the parts of an assembly line in an industrial plant, but in such a case moving ob-

jects or workers would probably give you a chance to
pan by following action—always more desirable than
panning a static subject.

If, also, you wish to emphasize the height of a building, you can pan slowly from the foundation up to the
top. Take note that it is the *length* of the pan, *not the
angle,* that emphasizes the height of the building.

Another important use for panning is in taking mod-
erately long closeups while a subject is in motion.

When you are photographing scenery from a moving
train or boat, panning is quite automatic, since you
yourself are moving. In case you want to swing your
machine in a true pan, you should do so from forward
(that is, from the direction of travel) back, so that your
pan moves in the same direction in which the scenery
appears to be traveling.

It may be readily seen from these specialized cases
where panning a static scene is justified, that the cameraman has a very definite continuity idea in mind.
Panning a static scene should never be done just because you don't want to back off far enough to cover the
whole scene in one or more long shots.

THE "HOW" OF PANNING

No pan, no matter how justifiable or effective in
theory, is any good if badly done. Far better than a bad
pan is no pan at all, since a jerky, wavering, wildly racing shot will kill all interest in your picture, and send
your eyesore audience home fast.

The physical elements of a good pan are steadiness,
evenness, slowness. They must be carefully studied and

practiced, especially when shooting static subjects where the lack of these qualities becomes distressingly notice-able. A correctly used tripod will ensure these quali-ties. For the many pans that you may have to make with your camera held only in your hands, a good stance is all-important.

The stance for making a hand-held pan shot is iden-tical with the stance for making any hand-held shot.

CAMERA PRESSED AGAINST FOREHEAD OR CHEEKS AND HELD FIRMLY.

ARMS CLOSE TO BODY, ELBOWS AGAINST SIDES.

SWING FROM HEAD AND SHOULDERS DOWN THROUGH HIPS AND ANKLES.

FEET PLANTED FIRM-LY ON GROUND, POINTED IN DIRECTION OF WHERE PAN IS TO END.

Get a solid base, your feet firmly planted on the ground, spread apart, with your weight slightly forward. Either foot may be advanced for comfort. Ideally, your feet should be placed, before beginning the pan, so that they point in the direction of where the pan is expected to end.

Next, give the camera triangular support by holding your arms close to your body, digging your elbows into your stomach, and pressing the camera against your forehead and cheek. Not every camera permits the use of *both* arms and elbows this way—but one is always better than none.

When panning, swing not just from your head and shoulders, but all the way down, from hips and ankles. If a tripod is used, you must maintain a firm grip on the camera and your body should swivel as you follow the pan.

Evenness and *slowness* are not always possible when following *action* with a pan. In such shots as a bucking bronco at a rodeo, or the antics of the family dog as he plays with a ball, you have to pan fast or slow, change your rate of speed according to the behavior of your moving subject. Your audience will not be upset, because its attention is focused on the action and it has no chance to think of anything else. There is, however, *no* excuse for lack of *steadiness* in a pan, regardless of action or the absence of it. Steadiness is a "must" quality in panning. If you can't make a steady pan, don't pan, *don't!*

A pan must be *level* throughout, with neither a sideways nor an up-or-down movement at any point in the film, otherwise your audience will find itself looking cockeyed at the subject matter. You *may* have to pan up (this is known as "tilting") with your camera if you follow an airplane taking off; but here the action accounts for the tilt and the audience is not made conscious of any bad camera handling on your part.

An *even, constant rate* of panning is most important

for smoothness. Irregularities in the rate of panning will cause your picture to move across the screen in jerks and will immediately distract the audience from the action to the failings of the cameraman. Even if, when following action, you cannot maintain a constant rate of movement, you *can* speed it up or slow it down *smoothly*. If the action—such as the playful dog—stops momentarily, then you stop panning momentarily; but there is no excuse for lack of smoothness when the subject is in motion. Like steadiness, smoothness is a "must" quality in the pan. Make your pans smooth!

No matter how steady, even, or smooth a pan may be when shooting a static scene, it will be disastrous if it is not made *slowly*. If your subject is not in motion and you pan it quickly, it will be blurred. Of all the mechanical errors in panning, a fast pan, with resultant blurring of the scene, is the most common. Over-fast pans are myriad; an over-slow pan is a rarity indeed. Don't trust the judgment of your eye on the speed of a pan. No matter how slow you judge it to be, it will *invariably* appear faster on the screen. So when you get set to make your pan at the slowest speed you consider desirable, just lean over backward and deliberately make it even slower than that.

Furthermore, the apparent speed of the pan is very definitely affected by the distance between the camera and the subject. Avoid panning a *moving* subject when it is too close to the camera, for only the most exacting slowness of camera handling will keep the picture from flashing by on the screen. For the same reason, don't pan with a telephoto lens unless *following action,* for even the slowest speed will cause your scene to race by in a blurred cyclorama.

The physical qualities of a good pan are plainly not something to be picked up in a moment. Practice is essential. A useful habit to get into is to "dry run" your pan—to rehearse, without pressing the button, the movement your camera will make in the air. Figure how your pan *will end,* and adjust the preceding motion to that.

OTHER FACTORS

There are other factors which improve a well-made pan. The human eye usually looks at a scene from left to right, or from the bottom up. Pan and tilt that way, when the action allows. Of course, following action such as kids romping in a playground will cause you to switch directions. But when your audience is absorbed in the action, it will not be distracted by this fact.

By all means avoid "whitewashing" a static scene— slapping your camera back and forth as though you were using a paintbrush.

It is desirable when panning action to precede the actual pan with a brief, non-pan shot of the subject, and to follow up the pan immediately with a similar shot of the last scene, before stopping the camera. Thus if Betty runs after a ball, try to open the shooting with a steady, non-pan shot as she starts her sprint; pan her over to where she retrieves the ball; and end the sequence with another non-pan shot. These "before-and-after" non-pan shots give your audience a chance to see what is going on *before* the camera moves, and to orient itself again to the scene that *follows* the completion of the pan.

It is jarring to the audience to be switched abruptly from a still scene to an action pan or from an action pan to a still scene. But of the two faults, the latter is much worse and less excusable. Many a time it is impossible to inaugurate an action pan with a non-pan shot. This especially holds true when the action is uncontrolled—in a horse race or track meet, for instance, where your subjects are in high speed all the time. It is difficult to find an excuse, however, for not holding your camera motionless at the end of the pan. Either your subject will come to rest, or you can simply stop the pan and allow the action *to move out of the frame* while you hold your camera immobile. It is extremely upsetting to the audience to see something that is in full motion on the screen abruptly cut off in mid-action. Give action a clean exit, so that it disappears logically.

Even if an obstruction, such as a football spectator jumping up and down while you're panning a touchdown dash, momentarily cuts off your view, always follow through on your action; keep right on panning so that you will pick up the action again beyond the obstruction and hold it until it moves out of the frame.

This point is so important that we repeat: *Avoid cutting from an action pan to a still scene.* Let your action move out of the frame. You've surely seen many a good newsreel sequence of a horse race where the cameraman (stationed at the finish line) picked up the ponies in motion at the far end of the straightaway, panned them until they moved up opposite to him, held the camera steady as they crossed the finish line, then stopped it only *after* they had moved out of the frame.

When you get down to editing your film, you will thank yourself profusely for having followed through with your camera and allowed the action to move cleanly out of the frame.

PLAN YOUR PANS

As you pan action closer to you, it will naturally become larger, thus commanding more of your audience's attention. As you pan action away from you, it grows smaller, and there is an inevitable—if relatively slight —drop in audience interest. Therefore, try to plan your pans so that they reach their climax when the action fills the screen. Conversely, never—if you can help it—begin a pan at a ninety-degree angle to your subject. Start it from a narrow, acute angle.

A pan has "buildup" quality. It should gain in interest as it moves along and its conclusion should be its high point, its peak of action and excitement. Otherwise your audience will be let down. A racing pan is much more exciting if it picks up the horses at the beginning of the home stretch and reaches its climax as they cross the finish line, than if it starts with the finish of the race and follows through on the horses as they slow down and stop!

One criminal perversion of the pan is to use it just to cover a lot of ground while shifting from one point of interest to another—a mistake very often made in a scenic pan. Don't be led astray by the fallacy that this is the way the human eye operates when it looks from one thing to another. The eye does not truly pan—it *jumps* from one scene to another, skipping whatever is uninteresting during the jump. While it is in motion, it sees nothing it doesn't want to see. Let your glance shift from one corner to another of a strange room and try to remember just what you have seen in between!

CAUTION AGAIN!

We have granted the good points, the special usefulness of the pan. We endorse it with reluctance because, as this chapter has made plain, a well-made, well-thought-out pan is no easy matter. We reiterate: Better no pan at all than a bad pan. Remember, no picture ever suffered from a lack of pans as long as the action could be covered otherwise. And there are mighty few instances where the action could *not* be covered otherwise.

Have pity on your audience—approach the pan with caution and respect. Use it sparingly—no matter how well you do it.

SUMMARY

——The pan is a photographic hot potato whose indiscriminate, incorrect use is the most common fault of cameramen and an acute grievance of eyesore audiences.

——Panning does have its specialized uses, but the cameraman should very carefully learn when and how.

——The *when* of panning applies to following action or to photographing certain static scenes where the pan can make clearer either size or the relationship of parts.

——The *how* of panning requires steadiness of stance, keeping the camera level, moving it smoothly, evenly, and slowly. A pan is usually made from left to right, a "tilt" from bottom to top.

——Hold the camera steady for a moment before beginning and after ending a pan. If the action is not to be followed through, let it go cleanly out of the frame before stopping the camera.

——Avoid switching from an action pan to a still scene.

——The end of the pan is the climax of subject movement. It should also be the climax of interest. If possible, shoot the pan from the position where it will reach its climax. Make the beginning from an acute angle and pan it through until it fills the frame.

——Avoid whitewashing.

——Do not pan merely to avoid moving back far enough to get all the subject in the frame with a single long shot.

——A pan is never indispensable to a picture and a bad pan is much worse than no pan at all.

——Avoid panning if possible!

CHAPTER NINE

DIRECTIONAL CONTINUITY

CONSTANT SCREEN DIRECTION

The screen has unlimited power of illusion. But "illusion" is not far removed in sound or spelling from "confusion," and the unwary cameraman will often find his instrument prankishly playing tricks on his audience against his best wishes and intentions.

We have said before and resoundingly say again that the cameraman must enable his audience to see the action on-screen the way he—the cameraman—sees it in reality. He must continuously take into account the fact that what he sees *directly* with the freedom and mobility of his eyes, is seen at second hand by the audience on a screen of rigid dimensions. The eye can pick and choose, but the screen *imposes* its story on the audience.

This is the danger of screen illusion. It can make confusing little, simple acts which are never misconstrued by the human eye when it sees them in real life.

Take the matter of movement. You come across a

67

parade on an avenue in your home town, and the marchers move across your vision from *left* to *right*. You cross
the street and look back: the paraders march now from
right to *left*. This is perfectly understandable to you,
so understandable that you never stop to think consciously of it. Your mind has automatically taken into
account the shift in your position to a reverse angle of
view, from which things naturally take the opposite
aspect; you are fully aware that the parade is still moving in the same forward direction.

But if you were to make motion pictures of that
parade, first from one side of the street, and then from
the other, the marchers would appear to be moving in
exactly opposite directions on the street; the audience
could not help being somewhat bewildered, lacking an
explanation on the screen for the change.

The first answer to the problem presented by a confusing position change is: Avoid it. Do so by maintaining *constant screen direction*. If you shoot a sequence
of the marchers, keep them moving in the same direction in all shots. If they move initially from left to
right, keep all shots left to right; if they start from right
to left, keep all shots right to left. Try to avoid direction changes between shots.

The same logic applies to more intimate movie subjects. Take, as an example, Mother with little sister
Betty in the park playing with a ball. Mother sits on a
bench and Betty has just thrown the ball; you want to
shoot a sequence showing her going to get that ball
and returning to Mother with it. Change of direction

is obviously going to be involved, but you have no problem as long as you make sure your camera tells the whole story. You shoot an LS showing the two subjects and the start of the action, move in for an MS of Betty going after the ball, follow that with a CU cut-in of her hand grasping the ball, then move back to an MS showing her turning with the ball now in her hand, and finish the sequence with an LS of her coming back to Mother in the opposite direction. The CU cut-in and the following MS showing the turn are your key shots here; they reconcile the audience to the direction change; they are easy to make yet they would destroy the whole sequence if left out. The success of directional continuity depends very often on not neglecting elementary shots. *(See illustration facing page 72.)*

MASKING DIRECTION CHANGES

Trouble may arise, however, in sequences where the action moves only one way but where, in order to photograph the story properly, you cannot avoid shots with different screen directions.

It may happen in the case of the parade that colorful backgrounds on *both* sides of the street compel you to shoot from either side, with resultant changes in screen direction of the marchers. So again, on a boat trip down a river, your picture might show departure from a river town on one side and arrival at a river town on the *other* side. En route, you might wish to photograph interesting buildings or scenery on *either bank* or boats passing on *either side* of you.

Obviously, switching back and forth from one side to the other would make many changes of screen direction inevitable; confusion would be possible.

Confusion would be possible, but *not* inevitable. That same power of screen illusion which creates all this directional trouble now comes to the rescue. It can be applied to avoid confusion in several ways, but there is one technique that is far and away the best because it is most effective and most easily and universally used. That is *distraction*.

THE TECHNIQUE OF DISTRACTION

Using the versatile cinema tools of cut-in and cutaway, distraction exploits the continuity truism mentioned previously: An audience, always looking ahead to what is coming on the screen, rarely keeps in mind *more than one scene prior to the one it is looking at.*

The distraction technique separates scenes of a sequence which have conflicting screen directions by an intermediate shot—or shots (it is always better to have two or more instead of just one)—in which there is no cross-screen direction of movement.

If cut-ins are used, the shots can be head-ons, tail-aways, or both. The parade will serve as an example. You are shooting the procession as it passes from left to right when you notice you are on the same side of the street as the reviewing stand. Since your climactic scene is to be the marchers passing in front of this most important background, you must cross the street to shoot it. But a shot from that side would show the marchers moving from right to left. So, before changing over, you take a cut-in shot in which the screen direction is neutral.

You step into the gap between two groups of marchers and photograph either the first group from the rear as it moves *away* from the camera, or the second group from the front as it moves *toward* the camera. In these shots the marchers do not have cross-screen direction; your audience ceases to be conscious of any such direction; and the climactic shot may therefore be taken without confusion from the other side of the street and show a right-left direction.

Cut-aways, similarly used, produce the same distraction even more effectively, because their subject, although related to the main action, *is completely separate from it.*

In the case of the parade, cut-aways may consist of spectators, of confetti raining down from the buildings, of flags flying along the line of march. Such shots take your audience eye completely away from the parade and the direction in which it is moving. If you then switch back to the parade from a different side of the street, your audience is not confused because it will have forgotten the original screen direction.

The boat-trip example has plenty of opportunities for cut-away distraction shots in closeups of passengers, of sailors, of boat-details like pennants flying, hawsers being hauled in and carefully piled, furrows cut in the water by the ship's prow.

(To avoid a troublesome misconception in the reader's mind, we wish to bring out here an important point that is properly a function of *editing*.

It is not necessary to shoot distraction shots *in the exact order in which they appear on the screen.* It might prove to be much easier, much more convenient to film the spectators or the flags at the parade after all the marchers have passed; or the details aboard ship at the beginning or end of the trip. The important thing is that when the film is finally edited, the distraction scenes be cut into the action where they may do their duty of masking changes of screen direction. The end product—*what the audience sees on the screen*—is the all-important thing.)

OTHER METHODS

The resources of screen illusion can be applied in specialized cases to *deceiving* an audience into accepting a reversal of screen direction.

An example is the boat trip down the river where you constantly have to switch the camera from one bank to the other. Ask some lens-struck spectator (whom you're sure to find in any situation!) to pose as an actor for you. Frame him in the foreground as he looks over the rail at the river bank which is moving by from *left* to *right.*

Now ask your actor to turn his head so that his gaze shifts to the other side. Shoot his action with the camera. That simple action of turning his head has *suggested* a change of direction. You can now shoot the other bank of the river from *right* to *left* and your audience will accept the reversal contentedly.

Still another way of keeping your audience satisfied

CHANGE OF
SCREEN DIRECTION
(Wherein the action
explains the change)

Left, Top to Bottom

Establishing Shot

Medium Shot

Closeup

Medium Shot

Above

Reestablishing Shot

CONTRASTING
SCREEN DIRECTION
(To create suspense)

Left, Top to Bottom

LS (Aunt Sally, r. to l.)

LS (Junior, l. to r.)

MS (Aunt Sally, r. to l.)

MS (Junior, l. to r.)

Above

Reestablishing Shot

(climaxing sequence)

about screen direction is to keep the same landmark, symbol, or object in the background in successive shots with different screen directions, so that its position in regard to the action keeps the direction of movement clear.

To illustrate: You are shooting a sequence of Mother clipping roses from a bush in front of the house. Mr. Montgomery, your neighbor, walks by from *right* to *left*. He is dressed carefully, his step is brisk, he is very, very definitely *going somewhere*.

When he sees Mother, however, he stops for a moment to say hello and to admire the roses. On the spur of the moment you decide to "shoot him into the story." Your establishing shot was from out in the street, with the rosebush *behind* Mr. Montgomery. It is to his right, in the direction from which he has come.

You close in for MS's and CU's, but to get a fresh angle and to fill up your background as much as possible with that handsome rosebush, you change to a shooting position on the lawn, on the other side of Mr. Montgomery. The rosebush is now on his left.

Mr. Montgomery is in very much of a hurry, unfortunately, and waits only until you finish your MS before he rushes off. As he leaves, you manage to pan him away and let him walk out of the frame, but now his screen direction is from *left* to *right*. There has been no time for distraction cut-ins, no time to switch back to your original angle from the street.

But the rosebush is *still behind him*. He has had his back to it consistently while he spoke to Mother, and the audience will know that he has not changed but is moving in one constant direction all the time—*away* from the rosebush.

The use of this method of masking direction changes is limited, of course, to scenes where a prominent, recognizable object is consistently to be seen and where the position of that object relative to the action helps keep direction clear. It would do no good at all to have a conspicuous building or landmark in the background if the action inexplicably moved first one way, then another, in front of it.

A sensitivity to screen direction is one of the refinements of good continuity and helps differentiate between the button-pusher and the trained cameraman.

DIRECTIONAL CONTINUITY IN TRAVEL SEQUENCES

Whenever a considerable amount of travel is being recorded on film, directional continuity becomes more important than ever. This is not only because you must avoid confusing your audience about *which way you are going,* but also because you have to convince it that *you are getting there.*

If you film your own travelogue of a vacation trip from New York City to the Grand Canyon, the same screen direction should be maintained regardless of the time interval between shots.

Let's say you're shooting your arrival at, and departure from, a picturesque lodge where you stay overnight en route. You shoot the car as your wife drives it up to the lodge entrance from left to right. Next morning, when your wife drives off, make sure that she goes out of the frame *to the right.* If she drives off to the left—in the opposite direction—the audience will feel that you are going back to where you came from. The actual time interval between shots was many hours; on-screen it is no more than a split second. That is how celluloid gremlins make illusion work the wrong way.

So great is the power of movie suggestion that sometimes you must "cheat" on the truth about screen direction. In this particular example, to get to the main highway again and resume your trip, you may *actually* have to retrace your entrance and drive off *to the left.* But if you filmed the truth, your audience would get the feeling that you were going back where you came from. Therefore, rather than go through all the trouble of explaining to your audience that you are *not* going back where you came from but are reversing direction *only momentarily* in order to get to the main highway before resuming *true direction,* it is much easier simply to drive off *to the right in your film,* stop the camera, turn your car around, and proceed merrily on your way.

Regard for the power of movie suggestion applies even to insignificant-appearing details of screen direction. If you shoot an insert of a map as your wife's hand traces your route on it, then follow with a shot of the car actually en route, be sure that the screen direction of both your wife's hand and the moving car are identical. Even in small things you should keep the illusion of constant screen direction unruffled.

CONTRASTING SCREEN DIRECTION

A reasonable inference from this discussion of changes in screen direction is that the whole matter is a nuisance, and that our preoccupation with it is wholly negative—to prevent audience confusion.

Once again, however, we find a continuity cloud that has a silver lining. Opposing screen directions *can* be used for positive purposes and do not present merely a negative problem. When different actors or actions are involved, they can create a very powerful feeling of suspense.

This effect is brought about by *contrasting* screen directions. Suppose you want to show two persons approaching each other. Their meeting will be the climax of the sequence. You want to build up to that climax; make the audience look forward to it eagerly, expectantly. Aunt Sally, for example, is coming to visit you. You wish to show Junior walking down the street to meet her, eager to see what toy or candy she has brought this time.

Simple and obvious as this story is, you can easily build up real audience suspense by individual shots of each subject moving in opposite or contrasting directions.

First you shoot an LS of Aunt Sally approaching from right to left, followed by an LS of Junior as he looks expectantly off-screen to the right and starts to move in that direction. Next you take an MS of Aunt Sally waving and moving closer from right to left, and then one of Junior picking up speed from left to right.

If you wish, you can add separate closeups with each subject still moving in contrasting directions. Finally, in a reestablishing shot, you hit the grand climax as the two meet and Aunt Sally lifts and swings Junior in her arms. *(See illustration facing page 73.)*

Although Junior and Aunt Sally do not actually come together until the final scene, the contrasting screen directions of each give the audience a mounting anticipation of that coming-together. The alternating, increasingly close shots produce a feeling of excitement the audience will not experience if you shoot the entire sequence with both subjects on the screen at the same time.

This method of creating suspense is an old movie standby. It is used to create a feeling of fearful expectation in murder movies: the killer is shown stalking through the shadows from one direction in one scene, while in the next his unknowing victim appears moving toward him the opposite way.

Every "horse opera" with its big climax of cowboys racing toward a meeting with a horde of Indians uses contrasting screen direction to build up the feeling of inevitable clash. With cowboys coming from left to right and Indians from right to left, the audience knows they are bound to meet. Excitement mounts accordingly.

But note—and note carefully—that constant screen direction is maintained for each subject. The cowboys, whenever they appear on the screen, are *always* coming from left to right, and the Indians *always* from right to left. If this constancy were violated, if in one shot the

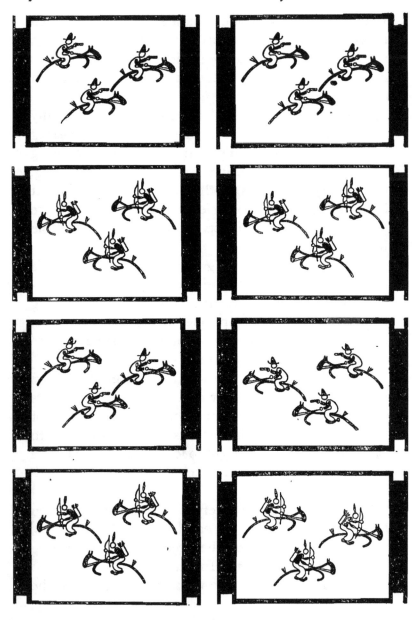

Indians were shown moving from *left* to *right,* the audience impression would no longer be that they were running headlong toward a clash, but that they were running away, trying to escape from the cowboys!

And the confusion would become indescribable if directions were continually changed back and forth, both for the cowboys and the Indians. The audience could not be blamed for bewilderedly concluding that there were not two but a half-dozen different groups, chasing and fleeing from each other all over the map.

So when using *contrasting* screen direction, make sure your individual actions maintain *constant* screen direction. The idea is to create suspense, not confusion.

CLEAN ENTRANCES AND EXITS

If you sat in the living room, closed your eyes for a moment, then opened them to find one of the family sitting in a hitherto vacant chair, you would certainly be startled. You would pop out with the question: "How did you get there!" Your surprise would be involuntary even though a moment's reflection would tell you that the member of the family had simply walked in.

A reaction of surprise would be just as inevitable if you closed your eyes again, and found on opening them once more that the occupant of the chair had vanished.

This shock of surprise affects a movie audience just as strongly when someone suddenly appears or disappears on the screen without the action's being accounted for. The cameraman may get away with popping people on and off the screen without explanation in trick photography whose purpose is deliberately to puzzle or dumb-found the audience. Pictorial continuity, however, has just the opposite objective. In the normal film, there-fore, where clarity and cohesion are sought, a person on-screen should be shown *coming from somewhere* when he arrives on the scene and *going somewhere* when he departs from the scene.

The necessity for this seems childishly self-evident. It is *not* self-evident on the screen unless your actor makes clean screen exits and entrances.

If you're shooting a christening in the family and want to make a sequence of Uncle Hal congratulating the beaming parents, let him make a complete, clean entrance by coming in from outside the frame. The same goes for his departure. Let him leave the scene by walking completely, cleanly out of the frame.

However—and this is a very important "however"—clean screen exits and entrances are imperative only when the presence of the actor concerned has not been registered in the establishing scene. If, for instance, in the opening scene of the movie you show Uncle Hal *al-ready* talking to the happy parents, his presence is es-tablished; the audience accepts him the same way it as-sumes that an actor it sees onstage in a play when the curtain rises has *already* made a logical entrance. Nor does Uncle Hal have to make a clean entrance if you precede his MS or CU by an LS showing him in a group of guests being greeted by the parents; his presence is established by the group shot.

The same logic applies to clean exits. Uncle Hal

need not move individually out of the frame unless the very next shot shows the group without Uncle Hal. In that case you have to walk him out to explain his disappearance.

Whenever you shoot clean screen entrances and exits, make sure they are really *clean*. That is to say, if you want a clean entrance of Uncle Hal, don't skimp on film by waiting for him to enter the frame of your viewfinder before starting to shoot. Let him come in cleanly from outside the frame. The same goes for his departure. When he takes leave of his hosts, don't stop shooting just as he approaches the other side of the frame.

Clean screen entrances and exits eliminate awkwardness and are always more dramatic. The extent to which they affect smoothness of continuity was stressed in our discussion of panning, where we saw that there was a distressing jump in the action whenever it did not go cleanly out of the frame.

Actors in a stage play make clean-cut entrances and exits. Let your movie subjects do the same. They do not have to come through a door, window, or gate as a stage actor must; they need only come from beyond the screen boundary—and go out beyond it.

CLEANNESS THROUGH MECHANICAL EFFECTS

Clean entrances and clean exits can be implied by the use of certain mechanical effects to make transitions between sequences. These effects, whose names are very nearly self-explanatory, are *fade-ins, fade-outs, dis-*

solves, blur pans, and *wipes.* All of them, excepting complicated wipes, are within range of the camera facilities available to the average photographer.

In a *fade-out,* the scene progressively darkens until it becomes completely black. It clearly implies the end of a sequence, whether the action moves out of the frame or remains within it. Aunt Sally's departure after paying Mother a visit would be definitely understood whether you faded out on her standing in the doorway saying goodbye to Mother or actually walking down the steps to the gate. The finality of her departure is clearly implied by the fade-out even though she does not move out of the frame in a true clean exit.

A *fade-in* is the exact opposite of the fade-out and carries with it the idea of a clean entrance. To suggest Aunt Sally's arrival you could fade in on her as she stood in the doorway greeting Mother. The fade-in as definitely implies arrival as the fade-out implies departure. If you wanted to emphasize the idea of her arrival even more strongly, you could fade in on her as she came up the steps to the door.

In a *dissolve,* one scene melts right into a following scene so that for an instant, before the new scene entirely replaces the old one, the audience gets the effect of a double exposure. The dissolve combines the ideas of clean exit and clean entrance implied separately by the fade-out and fade-in. In your sequence of Aunt Sally's arrival, you could use a dissolve by making a shot of her coming up the steps to be greeted by Mother, then running back the film and reshooting it on a new scene showing her sitting in the living room, chatting with Mother over a cup of tea. Thus in a sense you fade out on her coming to the door and fade in on her seated in the living room.

The *blur pan* (sometimes known professionally as a *slip pan*) is made by panning the camera from a normal scene with extreme rapidity, so fast that the subject is completely, unrecognizably blurred. Your next scene is shot in normal fashion. When you edit the film, you merely cut the new scene into the blur pan properly. For instance, you're doing a travel movie and want to exit out of a snowy Northern city and come in on a sunny Southern beach. Your first scene shows you loading your car in a snowstorm and driving off; suddenly it zooms into a blur pan which stops equally suddenly at a new scene showing you unloading the car in front of a hotel laid in a semitropical setting of bright sunshine and waving palm trees. When you edit the film, you simply cut the blur pan in between the two scenes to gain the desired effect.

In a *wipe,* one scene replaces another so that parts of both are on the screen simultaneously. There is no "blending" of scenes as in a dissolve; instead, the scenes appear adjacent to one another with clean-cut lines of demarcation between.

The most elementary wipe is the *push-off,* wherein one scene appears to be pushing off the preceding scene, with a frame line separating the two: Aunt Sally's arrival would be pushed off the screen by the living-room scene. This sort of simple wipe is within the range of the home cutter, but for more complicated ones, expensive optical devices and trained technicians are required. For these specialists there is no limit to the variety and complexity of wipes they can produce on request: spiral wipes, iris wipes, burst wipes, to mention but a few of the endless possibilities for design and dramatic effect.

Warning: These mechanical effects have the function of bridging sequences—they are transition shots. They should not be used as substitutes for clean entrances and exits between shots of a sequence. Their purpose is to connect sequences smoothly. The idea of clean entrances and exits which they imply is secondary.

It would be silly if you faded in and out between shots of Aunt Sally saying her farewells to each member of the family, or faded out on her as she stood in the doorway saying goodbye and then faded in again as she went down the steps. The actual transition in time would not be great enough to justify the fades. The same is true of a dissolve, wipe, or blur pan.

Don't fritter away these camera effects. Hold back on them for those occasions when they can do the most for pictorial continuity.

SUMMARY

——Changes of screen direction, unaccounted for by the action, confuse the audience.

——This confusion can be avoided by maintaining constant screen direction: that is, by keeping the action on-screen moving consistently from left to right or from right to left.

——When it is impossible to avoid reversals of screen

direction unaccounted for by the action, changes of direction can be masked in several ways.

——One method, depending on *distraction*, draws the audience's attention away from the fact that a direction change has been made, by shooting the action in cut-ins, especially head-ons and tail-aways, so that no cross-screen direction of movement is apparent. Distraction can also be achieved through the use of cut-aways.

——Other methods of masking direction change include that of *deception*, which *suggests* change; and that of the use of the outstanding landmark or fixed background object.

——In travel movies, constant screen direction is necessary not only to make clear to the audience which way the subject is going, but also to convince it that the subject is getting there. Directional continuity must be maintained in *little* touches throughout the travel sequence.

——Opposing screen directions of different actors or actions create suspense by *contrast*.

——*Contrasting* screen direction is effective because *constant* screen direction is maintained for each subject. Violation of this constancy leads inevitably to confusion.

——Clean screen entrances and exits are important. Entering a scene, the subject should come cleanly into the frame from beyond it; leaving, he should go cleanly out of the frame. Audience surprise and confusion will result otherwise.

——Clean exits and entrances may be implied by

certain mechanical effects produced by the cameraman or cutter for transitions between sequences. These effects are known as fade-ins, fade-outs, dissolves, blur pans, and wipes. Wipes, however, demand the services of a specialist.

——The exits and entrances implied in the use of these effects are strictly secondary to their transition function. Such effects are *not* substitutes for complete clean entrances and exits.

CHAPTER TEN

BUILDUP

THE XYZ'S OF CONTINUITY

This chapter on *buildup* marks an important milestone along the route of continuity study, and we may well pause for a quick RS of the road we have just traveled.

Thus far we have been bowling along a pretty clearly marked highway, where deviations from the straight and narrow have been inadvisable. Up to this point we have talked in specific terms about the structure of the sequence, about the mechanics of smoothness, coherence, and camera logic. These have been highly practical, hard-and-fast matters, with pointers and warnings and rulings; they have been the fundamentals, the ABC's of pictorial continuity. Now come the XYZ's.

The road ahead is no longer straight or narrow or inadvisable to stray from. It is wide open—broad as the horizon. It has guides for you, the cameraman, but real progress will depend on your creative imagination, on your "feel" for motion pictures, on that intuitive extra something that can set your work apart.

We have studied pictorial continuity in terms of achieving smooth, coherent action. Now let us apply it to get good story coverage, to create audience interest, to inject variety and color into the trite and ordinary. Buildup is what does this. It puts the frosting on the movie cake.

We have described buildup by indirection, in terms of similes and metaphors. It cannot be contained in a rigid definition, but it may be broadly defined as *the use of incidental shots or sequences which are subordinate to the main action but round out a story by giving it meaning, clarity, suspense, and excitement.* Although such shots are but modifiers of the main action, they are truly indispensable to complete coverage.

That's quite a chunk of definition. Let's look at it in picture terms: a movie of a garden party.

Your main action is simple and clear and breaks up easily into sequences. Your first sequence establishes the locale—the back lawn, with its grass, flowers, summer furniture. People come into the scene. They are greeted, served refreshments, introduced to others. You make special sequences of the punch being served, of guests consuming sandwiches, of someone playing a musical instrument, of card games, the award of prizes, and finally, of the party breaking up.

You now have a simple story containing most of the action common to all garden parties. You are going to introduce buildup to round it out, pep it up. You will seek out revealing, colorful details, shoot lots of closeups.

In your opening sequence you make sure that you

Establishing Shot	Closeup
Medium Shot	Reestablishing Shot
Cut-in	Cut-in
Cut-in (See pages 95 and 96.)	Cut-away

Reestablishing Shot
Cut-in
Closeup
Reestablishing Shot

Cut-in
Cut-in
Reestablishing Shot
Cut-away

get shots which emphasize the gala nature of the event and the fact that it is a bright, sunshiny day. If there are flags or streamers, you take shots of them snapping in the breeze. You shoot the glasses neatly lined up by the punchbowl, the trays of cookies, candies, and sandwiches. You get quick shots of junior members of the family looking wide-eyed at the lavish preparations, of Mother hastily touching up decorations before the guests arrive.

With their arrival, you look for details of dress which command attention. Aunt Sally may be wearing a fantastic straw hat featuring a figure of a bird pecking at cherries. You make a big closeup of this, and perhaps precede—or follow—it by another CU of Junior's eyes popping at the sight. (This CU is known as a *reaction* shot because it is the direct result of the action of a preceding or following scene. A reaction shot is very good for building up dramatic interest. Having it precede the action which causes it is a simple device for creating suspense.)

Instead of shooting the arrival of each guest, you make a series of buildup inserts of Mother's hand (recognizable by its distinctive dress-sleeve and ring) shaking a variety of hands, easily identifiable as male, female, or child. This series of buildup shots suggests a number and variety of guests, saves film, and gives a new slant to the prosaic, everyday business of shaking hands. When courtly Uncle Hal kisses Mother's hand, you get a novel shot: Mother's hand is already in the viewfinder; in comes Uncle Hal's to grasp it, followed by his face as he puts his lips to her fingers.

In the refreshments sequence, you take pains to get full-frame, close CU's of the punch being poured; then, as a tray is passed and the glasses are removed from it one by one, you follow a particular glass with the camera, show it traveling up to a guest's mouth, being tipped over and emptied, and close with the satisfied expression of the drinker.

As for the musical sequence, a typical buildup would be shots of a player's hands as they thrum the ukulele strings or press the keys of an accordion.

For the card parties or games, you lay stress via closeups or angles on the tiny scenes or bits of action that give point and punch to the sequence: the winning card hand, a chess piece being moved on the board, the reactions of the players—one nervously puffing a cigarette, another wiping his glasses.

In your departure sequence, you pay attention to a lady carefully pinning her hat into her hair; Uncle Hal's spats, shoes, and the tip of his cane moving down the walk; the gate opening and closing as one by one the guests leave; wheels of different cars turning as they move away. Returning to the garden, you get buildup in the litter and disorder that characterize the end of a party: quick shots of the empty chairs, the drained punchbowl, the soiled plates, the dog getting an accumulation of scraps, Junior collecting debris, Mother in a house apron that contrasts sharply with her elegant party dress, concluding with shots of the flowers, now dull and indistinct in the fading light, and the streamers whose limpness and quiet suggest that they too are exhausted by the activities of the day.

This description of garden party buildup shots, long as it is, touches only the highlights, the more obvious examples of the buildup material contained in a familiar story. Most of your movies will be equally familiar ones: activities of family and friends in their homes, in the garden, on the tennis court, on picnics, at the beach.

All such subjects are commonplace, but the cameraman who learns to use buildup artfully can make them stimulating and engrossing. Familiar as they are, they can usually supply enough colorful detail and action to give you buildup material.

The poorest motion-picture story will always be improved by buildup. It is up to the cameraman to cultivate it carefully.

WHEN BUILDUP IS ESSENTIAL

The need for buildup is most acute when shooting a static subject where there is no movement of the main action in or out of the frame, or when shooting a story whose main action has already taken place.

Take, for an example, Baby's bath—an inevitable subject for a home movie. It has surefire material, but it is also a relatively static subject.

To keep it lively and varied, you must use a wide variety of buildup angles and cuts: a full-frame CU of the soap as Mother's hand reaches into the frame and picks it up; another full-screen closeup of Mother's hand as it adjusts the water temperature or scrubs Baby with a washcloth; Baby's feet kicking up a foamy sea in the tub; Baby's hands playing with rubber toys; Baby's grins and hand-clappings of pleasure.

If you combine this sequence with one on drying and dressing the baby, you reestablish first with an MS showing the transfer of the child from her bath to the top of the bathinette, and then give punch to the action with buildup shots of Baby being scrubbed dry, oil being poured and rubbed in, powder being sprinkled, diapering, pinning, and dressing. Attention is focused, by means of CU's and angles, on graphic details like the oil, powder, safety pins, along with the smiling reactions of Baby and Mother.

These brief scenes are not shot in any particular succession—there is no order of LS, MS, and CU to them —and they are used anywhere within your sequence. Also, they are very short scenes. Two or three used here and there in rapid succession will give the simple picture a snap and lift that are sure to bring "Oh!s" and "Ah!s" from your audience.

Buildup will do the same sort of job in filling out a story whose main action has already taken place. Suppose you hurry to a neighborhood fire, only to find that the firemen have it under control. Its most spectacular phase is over, but you can still make interesting sequences through the use of buildup.

This you find in shots of the occupants driven into the street clutching a few belongings (a chance for inserts) ; in details of charred debris from the burning building; in the police holding back the crowds; in ambulance attendants, the faces of the spectators, the activity of welfare organizations like the Salvation

Army handing out coffee and doughnuts, the action of the engine pump; in angle shots of firemen on ladders or spraying water, of firemen's hands coupling hose or turning a water hydrant valve, of the hose swelling as water surges through it.

It should be reiterated, emphatically, that such shots can be taken *any time* the opportunity arises, before, after, or in between the main action. As *editor* you can later place them in whatever part of the completed film you wish.

The main action must be caught on film the moment it takes place, for it is hardly likely, in such a wildly uncontrolled subject as a fire, to repeat itself. But there is much more flexibility in the matter of buildup shots; there are usually several opportunities to take the same buildup scene, and action is often controlled. And remember, no single one of your buildup shots is —unlike the main action—really indispensable. If you miss a good buildup scene and can't get another crack at it later on, you can usually find a different one just as interesting.

No camera subject, however seemingly poor, dull, or lifeless, is completely devoid of buildup material. It can be found even in an empty room. Returning to an earlier example, before Mr. Prospect enters his office, the camera can take the empty room and tell a full story about him by searching out the objects and knick-knacks on his desk alone.

In any scene, patience and an inquiring eye are bound to turn up promising shots. The important thing is to be on the lookout for them. They are what give originality to your picture and stamp it with *your* individuality as a cameraman.

BUILD UP ACTION SEQUENCES TOO!

We have said a good deal about building up ordinary, static—even dull subjects. Do not infer from this that lively subjects do not need buildup.

In the normal run of a photographer's luck, you are bound to run across subjects crammed with buildup material, running over with action, colorful detail, human interest. Yet even with rich subjects, the tendency is to err far more often in the direction of too little buildup than too much.

Even if you are lucky enough to catch that four-alarm fire just as the first wisps of smoke come drifting out of the building, you should not concentrate exclusively on the spectacular scenes of the fire at its height, with flames and smoke everywhere and firemen rescuing trapped occupants in breathtaking style. These are wonderful shots, of course, undeniably the high points of your picture, but in concentrating wholly on them you are likely to ignore those less breathtaking buildup shots—the belongings of the inhabitants, firemen handling the hose, the faces of spectators.

These spectacular shots are peak shots of the action, all right, but they are peak shots *by virtue of contrast* with the less spectacular buildup cuts, and you will be sadly disappointed with audience reaction if you show it only the former without the latter.

Your audience will gasp, no doubt, but it will also feel a definite letdown. People don't live with their emotions perpetually keyed to the high pitch your exciting shots demand. Your audience has to be aroused, informed, led up to a climax of feeling to match the climax of interest provided by your spectacular shots.

Avoid jumping straight into the heart of a film story; develop interest and comprehension; let your audience warm up first, by seeing buildup shots.

CUT-INS AND CUT-AWAYS IN FULL GLORY

The heart of buildup, the main sources of those incidental shots which are "subordinate to the main action but round out a story," are cut-ins and cut-aways.

We have defined and described them; we have seen them applied in directional continuity to mask direction changes; but it is now, in their buildup role, that cut-ins and cut-aways come into their real glory, and their endless varied uses are fully exploited.

A simple example shows how they contribute to buildup. Look at your own back yard, where Johnny is mowing the lawn and his chum Freddy is raking the grass and carrying it away.

You shoot a regular sequence to depict the main action, then shoot inserts of the lawnmower in operation, filling your frame with the moving wheels, the blades, the cut grass as it comes spurting from the machine. These inserts are the buildup, explaining the nature of the action more fully, invigorating it with intimate, graphic details. There is Johnny himself. There are opportunities for cut-ins of his hands guiding the mower, of his moccasin-shod feet as they follow the machine, of the Army emblem on the T-shirt he has preempted from his older brother, of his cheerful expression as he pauses a moment from work.

And take a look at Freddy. Both he, as a live actor, and the inanimate tools of his work—the rake and basket—offer excellent possibilities for buildup cut-ins. Get full-frame closeups of Freddy as he bends to his task, or make a shot of his shirt bunching around the waist. Shoot another sequence on Junior as he begins to tire, with CU's of his dragging feet and weary expression; then return to Freddy for a sequence on the new action of filling the basket, giving it color with inserts of the rake in action collecting a mound of grass, his hands dumping the grass into the basket, and the filled basket itself. *(See illustrations facing pages 88 and 89.)*

All these are buildup shots, lending color, humor, interesting detail to the bare bones of the main action.

Head-on and tail-away shots can add a sparkling note to buildup. They would be interesting novelty shots in the Johnny-Freddy sequence, *whether or not* they were used to mask changes in screen direction.

Cut-ins and cut-aways, head-ons and tail-aways, are a blessing to the newsreel editor. Through them he can build up even the briefest sequence into an acceptable picture story. You have undoubtedly seen numerous parades or dedication ceremonies in the newsreels, where stereotyped action was enlivened by cut-ins of the participants and cut-aways of the spectators.

In these pages, we have fitted cut-ins and cut-aways into their proper place in the subject of buildup. We will return early and repeatedly to them, for without them buildup is impossible.

ANGLES IN BUILDUP.

Angles have been recommended for their value in avoiding the continuity fault of jumpy action between shots as well as for the variety they bring to pictures. We now pay tribute to their services in buildup.

Shoot Johnny from a high angle looking down on him: his squat, foreshortened figure seems sunk into the ground, performing a piddling, dull, undramatic job. Or shoot him approaching from a distance at a flat, head-on angle; his progress seems slow, leisurely.

But shoot the boy from a low angle which frames him against the sky. Then he'll appear to be performing an exciting, herculean task. Or take a close shot from a right angle—he'll seem to zip through his job.

There is nothing quite like a change of angle in motion pictures to stimulate and sustain interest, to make something "new" out of a well-known, familiar subject —whether it is Dad smoking, Mother hanging out the wash, or Johnny simonizing the car.

In pictorial continuity there can be too much of a good thing. The human eye tires very easily of sameness. A change of angle gives it the stimulus it must repeatedly get to maintain attention.

This need is most compelling in a short series of cut-ins or cut-aways of the same action: they pall if seen more than once or twice from the same angle. If your first cut-in of Johnny's lawnmower throwing out grass is taken from the side, next try a tail-away rear view from the ground level, or shoot from above the mower looking down and back as the grass blades zip from the revolving shears.

These different angles, by constantly presenting new aspects of the same subject, keep building it up to ever higher levels of audience enjoyment.

Cut-ins, cut-aways, and angles: these are the guides to buildup.

JUGGLING TIME AND SPACE

One of the greatest enrichments cut-ins and cut-aways bring to buildup is the ability to juggle time and space. It is in this particular talent that the motion picture most brilliantly demonstrates its magical powers of illusion. No span of time or space is too great for it to bridge smoothly and convincingly, rapidly or slowly—as you wish!

How often have you seen cut-aways of falling calendar leaves or successive shots of the same clock to indicate the rapid passage of time? Or a clock used to make the passage of five minutes seem like hours, by means of constant, repeated cut-aways to the minute hand as it slowly crawls from point to point? Hundreds of thousands of miles are bridged by successive shots of a speedometer showing different readings, by cuts of auto wheels spinning rapidly, by the sight of different signposts, by passing from a shot of snowy mountains to a scene of sun-kissed shores!

Let's analyze this magical power in terms of the sequence on lawn-mowing. Suppose you want a "before and after" picture of the lawn. Your opening shot shows it wild and weedy; your closing shot pictures it neat and even, after Johnny has finished his manicuring job.

But a lot of lawn-mowing lies between those two shots—quite a bit of time and space have been covered. You haven't enough film to shoot all that grass-cutting, and what's more important, the action would eventually get repetitious and boring no matter what means you employed to distract the audience.

The solution lies in cut-ins of Johnny mowing and cut-aways of Freddy raking. You simply take these cuts and judiciously spread them among your shots of the main action, which consist of regular LS's and MS's of the boys busy at work. Then the whole cutting and raking operation, which actually takes an hour to perform, can be condensed to a minute of film, and your audience will have the impression of watching a full, complete lawn-mowing job. Cut-ins and cut-aways will have concealed the time lapses.

The psychological secret that explains the audience's acceptance of this quick passage of time is the (by now!) old continuity truism that an audience rarely thinks back beyond the scene prior to the one at which it is looking. Cut-ins and cut-aways provide interesting distraction from the main action. When you *do* return to the main action, your audience readily accepts the idea that a good many things have happened, that considerable time has passed and considerable ground has been covered in the interval.

If your opening shots showing Johnny starting the

mowing are followed by full-frame cut-ins of his moving feet—even though these scenes are short and few in number, say two or three—the audience will accept without protest a succeeding long or medium shot which shows Johnny far away from his starting point and with a great deal of the lawn already trimmed. Passage of time and space has been convincingly *implied*. By using cuts of this nature throughout the sequence, you carry your audience unjarred over big jumps in time and space up to the final scene, which shows the lawn completely cut and raked, and the boys walking off with their tools.

Cut-aways are even more effective than cut-ins for putting over such an illusion. The reason is that they depict a subject completely separate physically from the main action. Audience distraction, consequently, is more complete. The perfect cut-aways for your lawn-mowing movie would be shots of Mother smiling at the two landscape artists, or a cut of the dog frisking about.

It is worth remembering that the illusion is always greater if you use several short shots of a subject instead of one longer shot. Reflect that every time you change to a new shot—no matter how brief—you introduce a new idea into the mind of your audience. Each successive idea multiplies the sense of time and space passing by.

TIME-SPACE TRANSITIONS BY MECHANICAL EFFECTS

Transitions in space and time can be accomplished on film by the fade-out and fade-in, the dissolve, the wipe, and the blur pan. These effects were previously discussed in relation to clean exits and entrances, but their primary and most important use is to make time-space transitions.

A fade-out "closes up" and "locks" a scene with un-arguable finality, and a fade-in does the opposite. A considerable span of space and time can be covered between the two shots without disturbing the audience in the least, as long as there is a logical connection between them.

An example would be to fade out on the lawn-mowing movie with a shot of Mother giving Johnny and Freddy a bonus of fifty cents for their labors, then fade in to show the two capitalists relaxing in an ice-cream parlor, enjoying sodas with their well-earned spending money. Not only would the audience accept this swift passage of time and space, it would find the quick contrast between the boys' working and relaxing states amusing.

The same psychology applies to the dissolve. It could be used very nicely to bridge the shots between the final lawn scene and the ice-cream parlor. A dissolve is especially effective when used to show different time readings. Dissolving closeups of Mother's wrist-watch during the lawn-mowing movie could suggest the passage of considerable time.

The blur pan and wipe profit similarly by audience psychology. Either device could be used for that time and space transition of Johnny and Freddy from lawn to ice-cream parlor.

But be warned: Never overdo the use of these mechanical transition effects. They should be employed sparingly and judiciously. Like narration, like titles, they should be used to point up, to enhance the action, rather than to serve as "crutches" or tricks to conceal faulty and uninteresting continuity.

CURBING UNCONTROLLED ACTION

The cut-in and cut-away will come to your rescue on many an awkward, film-consuming occasion when the action is altogether uncontrolled or unpredictable.

Suppose you want to shoot Baby's first walk across the living-room floor, starting from Junior in one corner and ending (you hope) with Mother across the room. Past experience has shown you that Baby's walking attempts are full of hesitations and distractions. You can therefore save yourself a lot of film if; after shooting her as she starts out, you make full-frame cut-ins of her face or, still better, of her moving feet, plus cut-aways of Mother smiling encouragement, and full-frame CU's of Mother's hands held out beckoning the child; then stop and wait until she gets within arm's length of Mother before you start the camera again.

In this particular case, as in most sequences where buildup is used, such cut-ins or cut-aways can be shot either before, after, or during Baby's attempt to cross the room, and put in their proper order later on when you edit the film. Flexibility is one of the great beauties of the cut-in and cut-away.

Beware one thing: When using cuts of this type, watch your screen direction—in those closeups of Baby's feet, for instance. Make sure it is the *same* as the screen direction in the establishing shot.

SUSPENSE AND EXCITEMENT

Buildup can do remarkable things to audience emotions. One of its most valued abilities is to create curiosity, suspense, and excitement, to send a tingle up the spine, to cause the audience to watch the screen in fascination and wonder anxiously what will follow.

Contrasting screen direction is one way of building an atmosphere of anticipation, but *any action not immediately explainable to the audience will create suspense.*

Your audience will not mind—it will enjoy the puzzle—if you keep the question-mark element interesting, and explain it eventually in a satisfying manner.

Introducing a subject or part of a subject in a big closeup will always create suspense. (When using a CU deliberately for this purpose, let the scene run longer than usual—don't make a quick cut of it.) With this in mind, let us try reshooting that simple sequence of Mr. Prospect.

Instead of having an LS first, you shoot a big, frame-filling CU of Mr. Prospect's hands engaged in writing, or perhaps of his eyes staring into or beyond the camera. (Staring into the camera, even in a big, dominating closeup, is all right as long as the eyes do not betray *awareness of the camera.* In other words, the subject should "look right through it.") Your audience, seeing those tremendous CU's of hands or eyes would immediately ask: Whose are they? Just what are the eyes looking at? What are the hands writing?

In the LS and MS scenes that follow **you provide**

the explanation. As your camera falls back in order to show the relationship of those eyes or hands to the general scene, the audience sees that Mr. Prospect is reading a letter or writing a check.

Now the familiar routine of LS, MS, and CU is completely mixed up. But that order of shots has never been termed unchangeable. It *is* the best method of telling a simple story clearly.. But when you want to introduce suspense and excitement, it is perfectly allowable to juggle the order around.

Only don't sell suspense cheaply! In the case of Mr. Prospect, it's something of a letdown to find that those big, staring eyes in your closeup have been looking at nothing more exciting than a form letter. But should you follow that CU with an MS of him at his desk, still staring beyond the camera, and continue with a reverse-angle LS that reveals a salesman not pulling out his samples but standing in the doorway pointing a gun at Mr. Prospect, you have justifiably varied routine to create suspense!

Suspense can also be produced by the extreme opposite of violent action, by a scene without any action at all. Open your picture with a sleeping figure; you immediately create curiosity about who the person is, just where he is, and what he is doing there. Put a troubled or joyous expression on that sleeping person's face, and audience suspense soars as it looks forward to learning the reason for the expression.

You can have suspense without any actor in the scene at all. Open up with Mr. Prospect's office before anyone walks in; your audience looks forward to seeing what manner of person will enter. Move in on some specific object in that empty room, such as a pile of banknotes or a telegram on Mr. Prospect's desk. Audience suspense grows sharp in anticipation of the drama that will unfold when the objects are explained.

Suspense does not need the extreme of high drama to justify it. It is also well employed for humorous effect. Suppose you opened the lawn-mowing sequence with a cut-in of a pair of feet. They move slowly, wearily. They suggest the extreme exhaustion of a man who has been on his feet traveling for many hours and many miles—a hiker or a woodsman, perhaps a refugee or a criminal. Then you pull back the camera to an LS and those tired feet are disclosed as belonging to Johnny pushing the lawnmower. You've got a sure-fire laugh.

CONTRAST

Contrast—for drama or comedy—is heightened by those indefatigable cut-ins and cut-aways.

Are you planning to shoot a story about Junior donning his first pair of long pants? Since that particular action is the peak shot of your movie, you want to build it up, so you precede it with a sequence that graphically tells the story of Junior's growth, showing a series of short, contrasting cuts of his infant diapers laid out on a cradle, his baby rompers hung on a crib, his shorts and knickers spread on his bed, right on up to that glorious first pair of long trousers.

Do you want to do a sequence emphasizing the delicacy, the tiny size of Baby? Let Uncle Hal take her by the hand for a walk. Shoot cut-ins of her little fingers clasped in his huge fist, or her diminutive white shoe outlined against his massive brogans.

Is that lawnmower sequence short on humor? You can get a sure laugh by following a cut-in of the mower shearing the grass with a cut-away of Grandpa's razor as he draws it through the lather on his face.

Are you focusing on one of Cousin Robert's big, fat, odoriferous cigars? Follow it with a cut-away of a smoking factory chimney.

Contrast material is present in nearly every subject or action, a powerful challenge to the imaginative powers of the cameraman. It is a most rewarding challenge, though, not only for the personal satisfaction which effective use of contrast will give, but also for the pleasure it will bring an audience.

A movie audience is acutely susceptible to the power of suggestion. Contrast has a great deal of that power.

Don't be discouraged when you gamble on an effect of contrast that doesn't quite come off. That will happen occasionally; it's part of the price you must pay to gain experience. You'll learn by observing audience reaction. Once you have learned not to overreach yourself, and your contrast does come off successfully, the warm response it receives will more than compensate for any previous failures.

LIGHTING IN BUILDUP AND CONTINUITY

Neither this book on continuity nor this chapter on buildup would be quite complete without a word about lighting.

Lighting has strong dramatic value. Even such

simple shifts in light source as back-lighting or side-lighting give a more interesting picture than lighting from a flat angle.

The professional cinematographer, skilled in the intricacies of the craft, can manipulate the entire lighting scheme of a scene to express varying emotions that exert a powerful influence on a movie audience. Low-key lighting, with its pronounced contrast in light and shadow, creates a somber, intensely dramatic mood. High-key lighting, with its abundance of illumination, is conducive to a cheerful state of mind.

The non-professional should be extremely cautious about attempting to use lighting for buildup, especially in interior scenes. It is a true art, complicated and subtle, calling for study and experience. But fortunately for the non-professional, too short of time to delve into lighting profundities, most home subjects are of an outdoor nature. Fortunately too, the indoor movie themes are usually cheerful and pleasant, calling merely for adequate illumination to get a good exposure.

The great concern of the non-professional, therefore, should be *continuity of lighting*—making sure that the lighting of successive scenes is reasonably consistent.

If you shoot Baby toddling across the room, stop for cut-in shots of her moving feet, then take a final shot as she reaches the safe harbor of Mother's arms, make sure that the exposure in all scenes is identical.

Suppose, in that lawn-mowing epic, you wish to make a complete sequence of Freddy carrying a basket filled with cut grass over to a large disposal can and dumping it. If the sun is dodging in and out of clouds, wait to make your different shots in the sequence for those moments when the sun's brightness is about the same.

A similar reasoning holds true for the use of filters. If you make a dramatic low-angle shot of Freddy against the sky as he strains powerfully to lift the basket to his shoulder, keep the filter on your camera for all other shots of the sequence.

Be particularly careful, when your story supposedly covers a long period of time, that the lighting jibes with the facts. If you're making a comic movie of Johnny painting the doghouse and want to emphasize his extremely slow progress by frequent inserts of a wristwatch to show the lapse of many hours, don't let lighting betray you! The sun is always moving, and a sharp-eyed spectator in your audience would get mighty suspicious if he didn't see the shadow cast by the doghouse in a different place with each return to the main action. (One could get around the problem, of course, by shooting this particular story with fast film on a dull day when no shadows at all are cast.)

The question of the movement of the sun brings us to another important aspect of lighting continuity: consistency of the main source of light.

You are shooting Johnny as he lies on the lawn, relaxing from his arduous painting labors. Side light is striking his face, so that your LS and MS in this sequence show half his face in shadow. You move in for a CU from the same angle. This shot should show the same distribution of light and shadow. Don't have him turn between shots to get the light fully on both sides of his face unless you show the action. Unless your movie audience sees him make the move, the lighting inconsistency will be obvious. If you think the CU shows his face too dark on one side, go back and re-shoot your MS with his face more fully illumined, either by having him shift his position or by using a reflector.

Of course, when Johnny has resumed his work and is moving around once more, he will constantly keep shifting his position in regard to the light source; his *movement* will account for variations in the play of light on his person.

The temptation to overlook consistency of light source is especially tempting when shooting indoors with photofloods, where the photographer has complete control of his light sources and can shift them at will. You are shooting a sequence of Mother rocking Baby to sleep in her cradle. The main source of light is a photo-flood placed to favor Baby, with the result that Mother's face is partly in shadow during the LS and MS. Don't —if you take a big CU of her—shift your light so that her face is fully illumined unless the MS shows her moving into a more favorable position.

Consistency of the lighting source, in sum, calls for careful attention to the logical requirements of your story.

THE ULTIMATE COMPLIMENT

The ultimate compliment to be paid buildup is the fact that it gives the camera one of its rare opportunities to triumph over the human eye.

Buildup develops, controls, and speeds up interest in what the audience eye sees in a way that the human eye in real life simply cannot do as efficiently.

The eye in real life easily gets bored. It will look with interest at what it sees for the first time, but will soon wander off in search of something else when the object of its attention turns dull or repetitious. The human eye is constantly engaged—outside the theatre —in the task of *selecting* what is interesting from the many commonplace scenes it encounters every moment of the day.

Had your audience seen Johnny and Freddy at work in real life, it would have watched with interest those actions which were novel and seen for the first time: the mower in motion, the cut grass raked together. But the moment those actions were repeated more than once or twice—as they must be—its eye would instinctively wander off in search of something new to look at.

Shrewdly built-up continuity spares the audience this monotony of excessive repetition and avoids the real-life strain of searching for "something different" to see.

It does so by pre-selecting footage that is consistently new and interesting, by concentrating attention through vivid full-frame cut-ins and cut-aways on the important phases of an action, and, with a change of angle, by creating a fresh point of view and stimulating interest anew.

Here we see the triumph of illusion. Surely real life is never as consistently absorbing and free of ennui as motion-picture buildup can make it!

SUMMARY

——Buildup "makes" a picture by injecting variety and color into the trite and ordinary.

——Buildup is the use of incidental shots or sequences which are subordinate to the main action but which round out a story by giving it meaning, clarity, suspense, and excitement.

——The need for buildup is most acute when shooting a static subject where there is no movement in or out of the frame; or when shooting a story whose main action has already taken place.

——Action sequences, as well as static or dull subjects, must be built up. The full effect of exciting shots is lost unless audience anticipation is led up to them by means of buildup.

——Cut-ins and cut-aways are the core of buildup. They are its most important, its most flexible and richest source of material.

——Angles play an important part in buildup shots.

——The juggling of time and space is one of the great illusions buildup makes possible to motion pictures. Transitions in time and space can be accomplished mechanically through the fade-out and fade-in, dissolve, wipe, and blur pan.

——Buildup shots can create curiosity, suspense, and excitement. They can also tell a story through the power of suggestion implicit in contrast.

——The non-professional should be careful to maintain continuity of lighting.

——Buildup shots are highly flexible in their use.

They can be shot out of logical order and cut into the proper sequence later on when editing. No one buildup shot is indispensable.

———No camera subject is devoid of buildup material; no matter how poor it seems to be, patience and an inquiring eye will turn up likely shots.

———The ultimate compliment paid buildup is the fact that it can triumph over the human eye. It manages to do so by winnowing only what is interesting from the dull scenes the human eye sees every day, and by presenting only the most important phases of action on the screen.

CHAPTER ELEVEN

STORY AND EDITING

EDITORIAL JUDGMENT

It is not the province of this book to analyze scenario writing. We are studying pictorial continuity: those rules of structure, logic, and form which work to make a coherent motion-picture story regardless of the type of plot, much as certain rules of building construction are applied regardless of whether the building is a hotel or a garage.

But just as rules of building construction do control the flow and movement of people within a structure, so does pictorial continuity have a powerful effect on the development of any plot.

This held true even in the simple sequence of Mr. Prospect, where the most emphatic, intensifying shot—the CU—was reserved for his face. In other words, there was a rudimentary scenario entitled "Seeing Mr. Prospect," which reached its climax with the closeup. Pictorial continuity was thus closely integrated with story continuity.

As a further example of the logic and laws of common sense they both share, neither pictorial nor plot continuity would allow an LS of Mr. Prospect to be followed by an MS of a horse race and then a CU of Baby eating her cereal.

The above analogies are an elementary view of the correlation between pictorial and story continuity. But with that correlation made clear, we can look further into how pictorial continuity, broadening in scope as it progresses, now touches on a subject that strongly affects the shape and quality of a cameraman's work. That subject is his *editorial judgment*—his control over his picture from the viewpoints of form, emphasis, tempo, composition, and final touches.

ADVANCE PLANNING

The ideal motion picture would be subject to the absolute control of a photographer blessed with a complete shooting script which he could follow without the slightest deviation. Well, there "ain't no sech animule." Furthermore, a good many photographers don't want to be bothered with an elaborately detailed scenario. Shooting a picture—especially for the non-professional—is often a spontaneous act, done on impulse, done to seize an unusual, quickly passing opportunity. It would defeat the photographer's purpose and even sour his pleasure to be burdened with a minutely figured plan of action.

So when we recommend some sort of advance planning, we keep the needs of the quick-working type of photographer in mind. He needn't have a detailed scenario, highly desirable though that might be. He can shoot very effectively without any script at all— "off the cuff," as movie slang puts it—as long as he does *some mental picture planning in advance.*

What does this mean? Simply that the photographer, before he brings the camera viewfinder up to his eye, makes a mental list of those shots he needs to have his picture coherent and complete; fits in his long, medium, closeup, and reestablishing shots, cut-ins, and the rest according to the importance or dramatic interest of the action; and keeps this mental list fresh in his mind at least two or three shots ahead of the one he is actually taking.

"TICKET WINDOW . . .

Dad, restless on a sunny day in spring, grabs his camera and calls out: "Come on, Mother, let's get the kid and go to the lake."

As he drives off with his family, he is already planning his picture. "Well," he thinks to himself, "haven't done a movie about rowing on the lake. Believe I'll do a thorough job on it and start off with a sequence at the boathouse. . . .

"Let's see now. Think I'll stop on the way to the boathouse at that hill that looks down on the lake and take a real location shot. Then I'll take my regular establishing shot down by the lake from the side of the boathouse, showing part of the building, people lined up to hire boats, the boats moored to the dock, and people out on the lake. . . .

"Now I'll get into the meat of my sequence by moving up for an LS of the line with Junior—I'll build my story around him—making a clean entrance and getting in the line. Next, maybe an MS of the cashier selling a ticket to someone, followed by another medium of Junior waving back to Mother, then a cutaway shot of Mother waving back. If I cut back to an MS of Junior now, I can get away with showing him pretty close to the ticket window, thanks to those distraction shots. . . .

"Think I'll try some more cut-away stuff to get him even closer to the window. I'll make an MS of him looking back over his shoulder and putting his hand up to shade his eyes. Now I'll make a closeup of this action, then move back of him and let the camera see what he's looking at. That'll be the lake—a whole regatta of rowers with lots of color. That's swell buildup and I'll give it a nice long shot. . . .

"Time now to get back to the business of buying the ticket. I've set things so that I can show Junior moved all the way up to the ticket window, and no one will kick. So I'll reestablish with an MS as he steps forward, pulling out his money as he hands it through the window. . . .

"I can get the ticket man into the action with a CU showing him taking the money and stamping the time on a ticket—good idea to get an insert of the stamper doing the job—and I'm all set now for an MS from Junior's *other* side that'll show him taking the ticket. . . .

"Taking this shot from his other side lets me set up for an RS by reverse angle from the usual side. I'll get him as he walks away from the ticket office, stops to join Mother, then I'll pan them both as they walk off to the boats—and *this* time I'll stop the pan in time to let them move cleanly out of the frame! . . .

"That's plenty in the way of advance planning before I get there. I can decide on the shots for the next sequence after I finish shooting that one."

So much for Dad's "stream of consciousness" thoughts about what he plans to shoot. Let's assume that by means of the persuasiveness so valuable to a photographer, he gets the people in the line not to stare at the camera, persuades the ticket man to stamp Junior's ticket over again for an insert, and in general manages to shoot the sequence pretty much as he had planned it. He does decide to add a few cut-aways of attractive buildup subjects he finds in the line—a young service man and his girl, a pretty little boy dressed in a sailor suit waiting for his father, a kid munching popcorn and waving a balloon.

. . . AND ROWBOAT"

Dad does the same advance picture planning as he prepares to shoot his next sequence, which is to show Mother and Junior boarding a rowboat: His mental scenario breaks down something like this:

1. LS of Mother and Junior approaching rowboat, letting them come cleanly into frame or else dissolving them into head-on shot; then panning them as they come around side of boat and prepare to get in.

2. MS from different angle [Dad invariably shifts his angles] as Junior hands Mother into boat.

3. CU of Mother's smiling face.

4. MS to show boat rocking as Mother steps into it.

5. CU of Mother's face as smile gives way to gasp of consternation.

6. CU of Junior laughing at her startled expression.

7. MS of Junior placing foot on gunwale of boat in order to steady it.

8. CU cut-in of foot.

9. MS from boat to reestablish as Junior waves Mother to seat in stern.

10. CU of Mother seating herself and grasping sides of boat.

11. ECU of her hands holding on for dear life.

12. MS to reestablish as Junior gets into boat and sits down.

13. CU from dock as Junior pushes boat away from mooring and grasps oars.

14. ECU cut-in of hands grasping oars.

15. MS as he begins to row.

16. LS as he pulls boat away from dock into lake, out of the frame.

Dad knows that some of the CU's and inserts do not have to be shot in sequence as long as they are placed in sequence in the final editing. If he has to he can, for instance, shoot the cut-ins of Mother's hands grasping the sides of the boat, and of Junior's taking the oars, one after the other, with the boat firmly tied to the dock; he knows he will be able to put them in their proper place when the film is edited, so he makes the inserts at his convenience.

Once this sequence is shot, he continues his mental planning of the sequences that will be necessary to complete the picture, always leaving room for changing, omitting, or adding shots to suit the situation at the time that he is actually shooting . . . keeping his planning flexible.

TIPS ON ADVANCE PLANNING

Neither of the example sequences given above need be planned or shot as elaborately as described. Either or both of them could be condensed a great deal, with no loss of continuity, although they would not have quite as much buildup.

Dad might decide that the first sequence, being introductory, should move very quickly, and should be confined to the essentials of buying a ticket. He would therefore confine his picture planning of that sequence to no more than the following shots: a location shot, an LS of the ticket line which Junior leaves Mother to join, an MS picking up Junior as he moves to the window, and a CU showing him buying the ticket. A reestablishing shot panning Junior back to Mother and holding on them both as they walk down to the boat. would carry the action smoothly into the main boating sequence.

The important point is that whether advance picture

planning is done elaborately or not, *some measure* of it be undertaken.

Another important lesson may be drawn from the mental picture planning illustrated by Dad's boating sequences. The lesson is that such planning presupposes, first and foremost, *a clear idea* of what the cameraman is going to shoot, of what his climax will be, and of how he will build up to it.

Naturally this sort of spontaneous scenario planning is much easier with a controlled story in your own living room, or even a semi-controlled story like Dad's rowing picture, than with the wildly uncontrolled story of a raging fire.

But mental picture planning within a sequence is always possible *to some extent,* even when action is wholly uncontrolled. Firemen putting a hose into operation or hurrying up a ladder compose sequences that break down into separate scenes of LS's, MS's, CU's, and ECU's, despite their high speed of action. You can figure in advance on a long shot from across the street as the fire truck rolls up (entering the frame, if possible) ; then a medium shot as the firemen start to unroll the hose; closeups of the firemen; a reestablishing scene as they drag hose to the water pump; an MS as they start clamping it on; CU's and ECU's of the hose being tightened on the pump.

Similarly, a sequence built around the fire ladder could be tentatively broken down in advance into a long and medium shot of it being raised and placed against the wall; a closeup of the machinery performing the operation and another of the fireman at the controls; an RS of a fireman starting to mount the ladder; a cut-in of his feet as they go up the rungs; a long shot as he goes into a window.

Obviously, not all of these shots may be possible, especially the close-range, intimate CU's and ECU's. It must be a stern and carefully obeyed principle with you, as with all responsible cameramen, never to get in the way of people engaged in rescue work at the scene of a disaster. Long lenses, in such instances, can perform the function of close physical approach.

The point to be observed in these examples is that advance planning, no matter how subject to sudden change or cancelation, *can* be done. It is possible for you to *anticipate* scenes in uncontrolled action and this anticipation, even if unrealized, can serve as a rough guide in shooting.

Your ability to look ahead and anticipate stages of action is a great boon to lightning-quick picture planning. But don't forget that this ability derives from practice and experience.

Just as improvised picture planning is easier when the action is controlled rather than uncontrolled, so is it easier if your movie is brief. Shooting Cousin Robert smoking a cigar is far less complicated than exposing several reels of film on a four-alarm fire. Yet even with the latter, you can rectify your mistakes of editorial judgment before or during shooting by editing afterward.

Here's a final word on advance picture planning. Look at it this way: Mother finds that shopping for the day is usually more efficient if she plans a list, mental or written, of what she must get at the butcher's, the baker's, the grocer's. Such a list takes only a moment to make up. Advance picture planning need take no more time. The important thing is *to do it*. The habit of it will soon take hold.

Whether you figure out your shots on a mental slate, or scribble a few notes on memo paper, or prefer to work out an elaborate scenario, plan your work in advance as much as possible—before, during, and after shooting.

EDITORIAL JUDGMENT WHILE SHOOTING

Advance story planning is a vital aspect of editorial judgment. But the planning is still only a means to the shooting. The payoff of your work as a cameraman depends on those powers of camera judgment that put your individual stamp on a picture, that enable you to mark each shot with your own personality.

The answer to this "how," the guides to putting your creative powers to work on a movie, have been suggested in the study of buildup, where concrete details in the form of cuts, variety of angles, suspense, contrast, and so on were called for.

But there are other factors, less exact, more difficult to nail down, calling for a strong exercise of editorial judgment, that play an important point in the quality, the liveliness, the interest of your picture. One of the most elusive and critical of these is tempo.

TEMPO

Tempo, timing, or *pace* are synonymous movie terms that have a rather forbidding sound for the non-professional. The idea of tempo, however, is simple enough. It is the rate of movement, the relative speed or slowness of your motion-picture action. It is determined not only by the speed of the action itself, but also by the amount of footage you give it, and by the kind of buildup it receives in change of image size and angle.

Speed is accentuated by short shots, shots of great contrast. In that sequence of Aunt Sally and Junior approaching each other from opposite directions, if you make each shot a long one, their coming-together seems quite a leisurely affair; if you make the shots brief and snappy, they seem to rush together. In short, tempo can be controlled by the relative total length of the scene.

Change of speed *within a sequence* can be manipulated through the general rule of changes in image size and angle.

A progression of image sizes from smaller to larger increases tempo—sharpens the sense of things happening faster. You'll find this is so whether the sequence is a salesman's meeting with Mr. Prospect or a tense scene in a Hollywood thriller where the would-be murderer closes in on the hero and the audience sees his strained face and upraised knife in successive, ever-larger closeups.

As far as angles are concerned, the closer you make your angle of vision—the more oblique, the lower it is—the faster the action seems to be on-screen. This holds true regardless of just what your story happens to be, whether it is the meeting of Junior and Aunt Sally, or a parade, or a christening.

The tempo of a sequence *as a whole* can not only be controlled by the length of each scene and the tempo *within* the scene, but also by the cut-ins and cut-aways used in among the main shots.

Cut-ins usually heighten action more than cut-aways, since they are intimately connected with the main action rather than with a related one.

Again, length of cuts has a direct influence on the general tempo. A quick cut of horses' hooves, or shouting spectators at a race, conveys more speed and excitement than does a long one.

The nature of the subject likewise has a bearing on tempo. If you're shooting a sequence of Baby out for a ride in her carriage, you'll find that a cut-in of the turning wheel conveys a stronger sense of motion than a CU cut-in of Baby looking around—an action she might be performing from a stationary position.

Control of tempo through continuity is obviously very strong. Never make the mistake, however, of putting the cart before the horse and trying to force slow or fast tempo on a subject, instead of letting the nature of the subject determine the tempo. You cannot, for example, photograph a snappy basketball game at the same tempo as a picnic without getting a dull, disappointing movie. But in a swift basketball game, you *will* have intervals of slower action. The tempo for these slower-paced intervals should reflect the slowing down of the action. You can get your effect by making longer scenes of the players dribbling the ball or else by lengthening your cut-aways of spectators or substitutes and the coach watching the game.

Such a mixing of tempos is a great boon to your movie since it brings that wonderful quality of *variety* to it; a change of pace is as refreshing to your audience as a change of scene.

The meaning of tempo—and its application via pictorial continuity—is easy to grasp. There is no more esoteric mystery to it than there is to any of the other phases of motion-picture technique, even though it may be somewhat more subtle. As with those other phases, you will gain skill and sureness through experience and careful attention.

A really great sense of timing is a rare gift; a movie man born with it has been endowed with a touch of genius. But fortunately for most of us movie addicts who were born with only average talents, a sense of timing can be *developed* that will be thoroughly adequate.

COMPOSITION

Editorial judgment is also very strongly exercised in *composition,* another means whereby your camera personality can be reflected in the way you make your shots.

There is one fundamental fact about composition in *motion* pictures, however, that must be brought out and fully understood. The fundamental fact is that—unlike the subject of the still picture—the motion-picture subject is usually *in motion*. All considerations must therefore be subordinated to the main one of keeping the audience's attention consistently on the action. Your guiding thought in "composing" on that moving celluloid canvas must be to present that action to best advantage, to keep it clear and dominant.

You start, then—as long as your action really "moves" around and is not static—by keeping it fairly well centered on the screen, since the center is the natural focus of interest. This thought behooves you to be especially careful when panning action. It also calls for caution when shooting closeups, because of parallax. In CU's the position of the image in the viewfinder will not be identical with the position of the image in the lens, due to the different locations of these parts on the camera. Therefore, in order to center the image in the lens, it will be necessary to adjust it off center in your viewfinder.

Your next consideration must be not to cut off anything necessary to explain the action. If you shoot a hockey game, don't frame the players from the knees up without ever showing their feet, because it is their quickly moving feet which *explains* their rapid motion.

You *can* hold off showing their feet until the sequence is well underway. This delay, if not protracted too long, is an excellent suspense—and surprise—device. Suppose, for example, that your audience, after watching "hockey" players whiz around for a while, saw the scene lower suddenly and reveal that they were wearing roller skates.

Be sure in such a suspense-surprise sequence to use a closeup to reveal the feet. The revelation is the climax of the sequence and should have attention concentrated on it by means of a CU. If you used an LS to disclose their method of locomotion, the action of the game would dominate the shot and weaken the punch of discovering the roller skates.

The composition of action in closeups requires extra vigilance. Make a clean-cut job of telling your story. Let's return to that theme of Baby playing with a toy. Don't make a close shot which has most of Baby's face and part of her hands stretched out for the toy but which does not actually include the toy.

Pull back far enough to get the toy in the frame, since it is an integral part of the scene. Now if you want to emphasize the toy exclusively, come in for an ECU of it alone, held in her hands. Next shift to an ECU of Baby's face to get her happy expression. Then to reestablish, pull back to a different angle and shoot the entire action without cutting any essential part.

In other words, give each scene a strong, clearly defined center of interest; make each scene *clean cut.*

To keep each scene clean cut, care must be taken in the way parts of the body are cut off when you are shooting CU's and ECU's.

In the ECU of the toy in Baby's hands, try to avoid cutting off the hand across the fingers. Try to show the full length of fingers, or better still, the full hand; try to show *a complete part.*

As for the ECU of Baby's face, there is no objection to nipping off a bit of her topknot now and then with your top frame line; just don't let that frame-line "knife" slip and slice her horribly through the eyes. If she is unusually animated and her head keeps bobbing up and down, keep your camera far enough away so that the head does not move in and out of the frame repeatedly. It is distressing to see Baby being scalped again and again.

Thus far you have been composing scenes of moving action, and your main concern has been to frame it fully and clearly so that audience attention is held consistently upon the motion.

Other composition considerations are minor as long as the screen shows plenty of movement with dramatic interest; the audience eye will be riveted upon it and oblivious of anything else.

But you will inevitably have static scenes with virtually no motion by your subjects. It is in such cases that conventional considerations of composition can serve the action well, both by focusing attention on it and by eliminating or reducing distracting elements. What are these conventional procedures?

When action is static, placing the subject dead center in your viewfinder (and consequently, on the screen) is a bad way to focus attention on it, because it emphasizes its static nature. Some displacement off center is desirable. Remember that the eye usually travels from left to right and from bottom to top when viewing the screen, and spot your subject a little to the right and above center; this will tend to reduce its deadness, its static quality. Static action justifies—and allows time for—such finickiness.

To avoid the monotony created by an even balance, take pains in scenes which show the horizon to make sure that the horizon line crosses in the lower or higher third of the frame instead of exactly in the middle.

Furthermore, because the eye does travel from the bottom of the picture upward, minimize the foreground —unless your action or main subject is located in it. If you cannot avoid having your action take place at the top of the frame, leaving a large stretch of unimportant foreground or "waste space," try to utilize it so that it leads the eye to the subject; or else minimize it by reducing it or breaking it up, where possible, by the use of shadow.

For example, you are filming a long shot of worshippers entering a church on a hilltop, with much empty hillside in the foreground. Instead of resignedly shooting it that way, move around until your viewfinder frames the road winding up to the church and leading the eye right to it. Better still, wait until a car enters the frame and drives up the road. With action in it, your foreground is no longer waste space. Even if your shot has to show the church alone, with no one going up the hillside, you can break up that monotonous foreground by scouting out some natural object like trees or rocks which throw a shadow.

You can use waste foreground to excellent advantage by manipulating the camera so that some object in the near foreground becomes *part of the frame line,* replacing the rigid line of the viewfinder. The doorway could serve to frame the LS of Mr. Prospect's office. It may be seen, from this example, that a foreground object used for framing is not of great importance to the scene. It may be human or it may be inanimate. In either case, however, it serves the function of a prop which both eliminates waste space and draws the eye to the main subject by creating contrast and a feeling of depth.

If you were shooting that horse race, an excellent foreground frame could be found in a fence rail; a live prop could be found in the head and shoulders of a spectator. The human shape would not be in very sharp focus, but this would matter little since it would be recognizable in outline and would perform its framing function.

Framing can be done on the sides and background of your picture as well as the foreground. In that salesman's call on Mr. Prospect, the sides of the office doorway could be used as a frame. Employing tree branches to frame the background at the top of a scenic shot is another familiar device. Framing material can be found most anywhere: a lamp will serve when shooting a living-room scene, a bush when shooting scenery.

As for a good background, it should—at the least— be free of anything that distracts the audience from the main subject. Don't have either moving objects, such as a dog frisking around while you're shooting Aunt Sally spading her garden, or immobile objects, such as a tree directly behind her which seems to be sprouting right out of her hat.

A good background, at best, will cause your subject to stand out more prominently by virtue of contrast. Never forget the graphic powers of light and dark, and the desirability of setting off your subject against a background of contrasting tone. A blonde girl will stand out much more effectively than a brunette against the dark of a shadowed doorway; equally, the brunette will photograph better against the white-painted wall of a house.

The audience eye, by the way, is attracted to light tones before dark tones. (This may well be one of the reasons why gentlemen prefer blondes.)

We have here given a resume of the important considerations of composition in so far as they affect moving pictures. We are frankly reluctant to dwell on the subject, because composition comes more and more into its own as action becomes increasingly static—in effect, less and less of a motion picture. It comes most fully into its own when shooting scenery, which is where the motion picture comes closest to the still picture. Motion-picture photographers too entranced by static composition possibilities sometimes forget the importance of action.

AFTER THE SHOOTING IS OVER: EDITING

Editing is the final stage in the study of pictorial continuity. It is only when you take your finger off the button after the final shot that you can really assess your work, smooth out the rough spots and polish up the good points.

Theoretically, final editing can be dispensed with when you have ideal shooting conditions: complete control and a detailed script. In such cases you can shoot your scenes with such precision that virtually no cutting or editing (the terms can be considered synonymous) will be necessary afterward. This is known as *cutting in the camera.*

Cutting in the camera, like any state of perfection, can never be more than partly realized. Even in Hollywood, where shooting conditions come nearest to perfect control, there is a colossal amount of waste footage. Despite minutest care in advance planning, and the most costly preparations, the job of editing a Hollywood film after it is completed is almost as big as the job of shooting it.

In actual truth, you—the non-professional or the beginner—can come nearer than Hollywood to cutting in the camera, because your picture plan is likely to be far more simple. But you too will inevitably have to do some final editing.

Film with mechanical faults such as edge fog, scenes where the subject gawked into the camera, scenes which were subsequently reshot because a better angle was discovered—all will have to come out.

Such deletions are obvious and inevitable. What is most important about final editing, what indeed makes it almost *mandatory*, is that you have an opportunity to look at your film the way the audience will see it. You get an exclusive preview, you have a chance to see how close you came to achieving the objective you were shooting for, you have the opportunity to cut out poor footage, to rearrange scenes for better continuity and dramatic effect, to tinker with tempo, reshoot where necessary—in general, you can polish your work as near to perfection as possible.

If you have shot a considerable number of cuts, editing gives you a chance to put them in their proper order. Recall how, in those example sequences when shooting uncontrolled action that was moving fast— the horse race, the fire—you grabbed the most exciting shots first before they were no longer available, then took the buildup shots with greater leisure and care. Their being jumbled up in the camera didn't matter; you knew you could arrange them for continuity in the final editing.

There will be many times when you will finish shooting one movie story on the beginning of a roll of film, and start shooting another on the same roll. There will be times when you take various shots or sequences at random, to use in a more elaborate, fully planned movie story later on. In all such cases, the non-related shots will have to be cut out and filed separately.

Still another reason for final editing is the fact that it is wise, when shooting, to make your scenes a little long. The cautious cameraman will start his camera rolling just before his action begins and keep shooting for an instant after the action ends. You should not only make sure of getting the complete picture, but have additional frames for overlap or any other splicing contingencies. Always bear in mind the continuity truism that one cannot put into a film while editing what was not registered on film when shooting.

As for tempo, editing gives you a shining opportunity to put into your picture more snap and speed where called for, or to pace it at a more tranquil rate of movement when that is appropriate. You can edit your film for tempo by trimming overlong scenes, by inserting cut-ins and cut-aways to get varied effects. Remember that there isn't too much danger of making your shots too short when editing for tempo. It is a far more common fault for movies to drag than to move too briskly.

IS IT REALLY WASTE?

The idea of throwing away film tends to hurt the non-professional in pride and purse—he thinks. It will reassure him to know that every experienced cameraman figures on a margin of waste. It is inevitable.

Far more film is left on Hollywood cutting-room floors than ever appears in the local theatre. The ratio of discarded to used footage may run as high as ten to one. Even newsreels usually shoot several hundred per cent more film than is actually used. The non-professional cameraman therefore need not feel he is throwing his money away if the exigencies of good continuity require him to discard ten per cent of his film!

So don't worry about those trims you throw away. What seems like wasting film is actually conserving—conserving the quality of your motion picture.

DO YOUR OWN EDITING!

A good many non-professional motion-picture cameramen do not do their own editing. Many beginners —or even seasoned non-professionals—are reluctant to do so; they may lack the equipment, the time, feel they require special technical knowledge, or simply prefer to have their films edited "outside" by a professional outfit.

Shortage of equipment constituted a valid excuse for a while, but the wartime drought has been assuaged and the editing tools—the splicers, rewind wheels, light tables, and the rest—are coming on the market in abundant quantity. As for the mechanical technique required to use this equipment, it will take the non-professional no longer to learn to handle shears and splicer than it took him to learn how to load a camera and set exposure and focus!

We find it a sorry thought that a cameraman who has conceived, planned, and photographed a movie story, however simple, could let a total stranger do the final editing. Allowing such a thing to happen to his "brain-child" is like bringing a flesh-and-blood child into the world and turning him over to someone else to be raised!

Your picture is your creation, *your* "baby." Don't give it away to someone who cannot understand your ideas and hopes for it.

Edit your film yourself. Having done that in addition to planning your story, directing, and shooting it, you may deservedly assume the title of producer, too!

SUMMARY

——Pictorial continuity has a strong influence on the form and internal structure of a motion-picture story.

——This influence is expressed through the editorial judgment of the photographer.

——Editorial judgment is exercised before shooting by means of *advance planning*.

——*Some* advance planning is desirable, whether it is a detailed scenario or a few mental notes.

——Editorial judgment exercised *during* shooting stamps the cameraman's individuality on each scene.

——Such factors as tempo and composition call for editorial judgment during shooting, as well as buildup methods.

——Tempo determines the speed at which the story seems to move; it is affected by length of shots, rate of movement of action, angles, use of cut-ins and cut-aways.

——The primary consideration of good composition in a *motion* picture is to focus attention on the main action, and to eliminate or reduce distracting elements.

——The final expression of editorial judgment is in the editing of the film after shooting—in placing cut-ins, cut-aways, and other shots in their proper order, in matching action through overlap, in eliminating bad scenes and bad film, in adjusting tempo, and in many other essential operations.

——Any waste incurred through the throwing away of film is more than compensated for by the saving of film quality.

——There is little excuse for the non-professional's refraining from doing his own editing: the wartime shortage of editing equipment is over; there is no special mechanical technique to be learned; and finally, the cameraman is definitely unfair to his own creative effort when he turns over the editing of his movie to a professional who is a stranger to his own conception of that movie.

CHAPTER TWELVE

CAN YOU DO IT?

QUESTIONS BEFORE THE HOUSE

It is now, in the closing phase of our study, that we can fully appreciate how closely knit is the interrelationship of all the aspects of continuity; how this advanced chapter is intimately related to the elementary one about the basic shots of the sequence, and both subjects to the chapters in between; how a single shot should be considered—*at one and the same time*—in terms of all the various factors of continuity. The whole of continuity is, indeed, equal to the sum of its parts.

The reader, however, may sigh at the abundance and variety of things the full use of continuity requires— the special shots to take, the cut-ins and cut-aways, the things to watch out for, screen direction, clean exits and entrances, and so on and on and on. All to make a simple home movie.

You may be convinced of your ability to handle continuity from the viewpoint of ideas or technique, but you may at the same time wonder whether you can afford enough film for all the various continuity touches. "Doesn't it require far more footage," you may ask, "than if I just aimed the camera from one or two positions and banged away, getting everything in with one or two shots?"

The answer is unequivocally "No!" The motion-picture shots of the average non-professional are individually much too long. He will start his camera from one position and simply let it run on far longer than necessary to get that one scene over to the audience. The unnecessarily exposed film in any one of these overlong shots would easily be adequate for breaking it down into separate scenes, with cut-ins and cut-aways, overlap, and other refinements of continuity.

It is a common fault of a cameraman untrained in the uses of continuity to expose twenty feet or more in a single shot from the same position—as, for instance, in a sequence showing the family gathered around Junior's birthday cake. He lets his camera run on, he explains, because "I can get almost everybody in from this spot and since there are quite a few people in the scene, I want to let the shot run long enough so that the audience has a chance to see everyone." ! ! !

Then—since a few people *were* left out—he moves his camera to an angle from where he can get *them* into the picture too, and makes another shot as long as the first or longer. He has by now exposed forty or fifty feet of film—of very dull film. (Much more than that, if he is using 35-mm. instead of 16- or 8-mm. film.)

How much better that picture will be if, with his first twenty feet, he shoots a real sequence: eight feet on an LS, five feet on an MS, a CU of Junior cutting the cake for another five feet, with a two-foot insert of the knife as it plunges through the frosting!

Then, with the remaining footage, he can still "get everybody in"—and make the picture far livelier—if he takes a reestablishing shot about seven feet long showing Junior handing out slices of cake, then several closeups, two or three feet each, showing the individual guests happily gorging themselves, and ends with a final LS—using what film remains—of Junior looking ruefully at the empty cake plate while his guests contentedly lick the crumbs!

The ultimate truth about applying continuity to a picture is this: Not only does it require *no more* than the ordinary amount of film, but it actually leads to more economical usage! The unplanned, blind act of just "shooting a roll" changes, through it, to a careful appraisal of scene lengths, to the use of proper tempo and emphasis for each shot.

YOU CAN'T ARGUE WITH ARITHMETIC

So remarkable can be the saving of film through such continuity devices as cut-ins and cut-aways that we wish to bring the point home once for all by means of a "master" example citing exact figures on footage per scene.

Our example is a movie showing a workman loading sand aboard a truck. Our cameraman is you.

You perceive at once that if you keep grinding the camera while the entire sandpile is being shoveled into the truck, you will bore your audience, declare a dividend for the film manufacturers—and in the end discard most of the film.

You are going to avoid this triple threat. Let's follow through on your shooting and see how.

First, you put the establishing shot to work and make an LS of the man as he attacks the sandpile with his shovel. You shoot exactly *six feet* of 16-mm. film. (16 mm. is a size the home cameraman will frequently use, and provides a good standard example here.)

Next you take an MS using *six feet* more.

Now you get going on cut-ins and cut-aways. You shoot a full-frame cut-in CU of the shovel as it digs into the sandpile and withdraws with its load out of the frame, comes back empty, is refilled, and goes out of the frame once more. *Four feet* of film have been used on this shot.

You change your angle completely for the next scene, but stay in close, almost filling the frame with the shovel. You repeat the action and show two more shovelfuls being removed; this requires another *four feet*.

For the next shot you change position and frame the view against the sky, with the edge of the truck just inside the frame. You shoot the shovel coming into the frame fully loaded with sand, and watch the sand leave the shovel and fall into the truck. You keep the camera motionless while the action is repeated (the empty frame between shovelfuls creates a slight pause which is buildup in itself) . Another *six feet* of film has been exposed.

At this point you switch camera position for a really low angle shot looking up into the perspiring face of the man. *Three feet* will suffice.

Now you give the camera and yourself a real rest. You sit down and wait until the truck is about half full. Then you find yourself a position for a nice high angle shot. From this new vantage point you make a reestablishing shot down on the half-filled truck and past it to the man in the background working on the now half-removed sandpile. *Six feet* of film is used.

Once more you take a break until the workman has only about three shovelfuls of sand left. Then you return to your original location and shoot him as he dumps the final loads aboard the truck and mops his brow. *Six feet* will cover the shot.

Check what you have shot thus far. In all, you have taken forty-one feet. Your action is complete, but to add a satisfying finishing touch you move across the street for a final LS showing the workman as he climbs aboard the truck and drives out of the frame. *Six feet* of film will be ample for this closing scene.

You now have *forty-seven feet.* When you edit this material and trim some of those four-foot-length CU's of the shovel digging into the sandpile, or the shovel's being unloaded into the truck (for the chances are far greater that you shot too much rather than too little) , you will find that your finished sequence cuts down to about forty-two feet, which will run on the screen for about seventy seconds.

The whole job of sand removal, an operation that actually took a half-hour, is run through on the screen in little over a minute—clearly, convincingly, *interestingly*, with no part of the story left untold, and with extreme economy of film!

Thus, to the question whether you have enough film to use pictorial continuity every time you shoot, the answer is emphatically, overwhelmingly—Yes!

HOW ABOUT STORY MATERIAL?

Another question that may be on your mind is: Do simple domestic picture subjects lend themselves to all these varied touches of good continuity?

The answer can easily be inferred from the illustrations we have used throughout; they have been drawn consistently from the personal environment and the daily affairs of almost any family.

There is no aspect of home life too small or too static to be built up into some kind of story. That is one of the great services of continuity—to take a subject which at first glance seems to offer opportunity for no more than a still-camera shot, and build it up into a genuine motion-picture story.

Any subject taken at random will lend itself to this treatment. Here, let's pick on you, the reader. What are you doing at this very moment? . . . reading this book. That might make a nice still shot. But it will do more—it will make a motion picture.

Surprising? Well, it can be done by applying the tricks of continuity. Here's how it might break down into a motion-picture sequence.

1. LS of living room with copy of this book on end-table next to easy chair. A few feet of this—then you, the reader, make clean entrance, walk over to chair, sit down.

2. MS from change of angle. Camera is moved in front of chair near floor and angled up at you as you stretch out, look down at table, see book.

3. CU from side angle near end-table with book in foreground as you stretch out hand, pick it up, look at it.

4. ECU cut-in, from over your shoulder, of book to show title.

5. CU of your face as you rub chin with hand speculatively.

6. LS to reestablish as you look up at clock on mantel over fireplace, then look down to book and begin to read.

7. CU cut-away to clock to show hands at one o'clock, then dissolve into . . .

8. . . . CU from another angle on clock showing time as three o'clock.

9. MS of you reading page near end of book.

10. MS from another angle as you close book, lay it on table.

11. LS from corner of room opposite to doorway as you rise, with camera panning you over to doorway. Out you go through doorway and out of the frame.

The sequence is finished. Using about half of a fifty-foot roll of 16-mm. film, a motion picture has been made out of a subject that at first glance seemed completely static and impossible of development as a motion-picture story.

But this is only scratching the surface of what can be done to build up the ordinary, everyday subject of reading a book. A sequence of you lighting a cigarette could be cut in, followed by a dissolve from a shot of one cigarette stub in the ashtray to a shot of a trayful of butts indicating the passage of time.

Still more meat could be added by a third sequence showing you putting the book face down when you reach the chapter on panning, getting out your camera, and practicing a pan. (This sequence, indeed, could very well be divided into two or more subordinate sequences.)

The movie could be given a comic twist by having Junior run back and forth with his toys, or chase the dog. Such a sequence would provide plenty of opportunity to apply the new knowledge of panning and directional continuity, with head-ons and tail-aways of Junior, cut-ins of his racing feet, cut-aways of the dog, and the like. Things could be worked up to a furious tempo by brief flashes of Junior dashing to and fro and quick cuts in between of your harried, exasperated expression.

Finally to put a good ending on the whole picture, there could be a sequence of you grabbing the book and your camera, clapping your hand on Junior's shoulder, pointing outdoors, and marching him off with the obvious intention of practicing a little of what you have been reading . . . so on out of the room in a nice fade.

Any subject at all is susceptible to treatment by pictorial continuity; conversely, pictorial continuity will build up a genuine motion picture out of any subject.

You certainly *can* do it!

SUMMARY

——The motion-picture cameraman can apply pictorial continuity to his work without using more film than he would otherwise.

——He need not be worried about whether home movie subjects lend themselves to continuity treatment; they most emphatically do, and are greatly enriched thereby.

CHAPTER THIRTEEN

IS IT WORTH IT?

STILL-PICTURE PSYCHOLOGY

The use of pictorial continuity is the secret of *good* movie-making. It is the easiest, simplest way, because it is the correct way. But—and this is a thankful thing —even the most expensive, gadget-studded movie camera hasn't got pictorial continuity built into it, to function automatically for the cameraman whenever he shoots a story. Continuity is what transforms a strip of exposed film into a motion picture; no gadget can do that. It calls for a little thought in advance, for a good deal of movement to and fro for different angles and shots, for care—deliberation—planning.

The question therefore arises, especially for the non-professional who does his shooting during a few precious hours of leisure: Is it worth it?

Wouldn't it be easier just to load one's camera, check focus and exposure, make sure composition and the expression of the subject are good—and just shoot? Just as one does with still pictures?

Just like still pictures! The ghost of still-picture psychology hovers around many beginning motion-picture cameramen—and logically, for most of us shot stills years before we took up the movie camera. So let's get the straight facts of the matter.

Operating a motion-picture camera with still-camera technique will get you pictures all right; if you are a competent still cameraman those pictures no doubt will be "good" in the sense of being well exposed, nice and sharp, probably well composed, even lively.

But without pictorial continuity, they will not be motion pictures. They will be animated still pictures. Perhaps you will be content to have them so. But we think it an awful shame if you ask of your motion-picture camera only what any decent still camera will give you—a good, sharp, pleasing likeness.

You will be unfair to the ability of the motion-picture camera to do more than just render a likeness; you will be ignoring its power to tell a living story.

You will also be unfair to yourself, because the apparent trouble of breaking down action into sequences, and sequences into separate shots, the "bother" of observing pictorial continuity, are really no problems at all, but add immeasurably to the sheer fun of movie-making. Once you try it, the bother of getting buildup shots, of establishing tempo, and so on, will warm you up, exhilarate you with an appeal to your imagination and your creative instinct—an instinct that is latent in every camera zealot.

Look at the question from the viewpoint of your prospective audience. Every moviegoer who has seen good and bad movies is sensitive to continuity. He may not be consciously aware of it—he may never even have heard of the term—but it has had its influence on him just the same.

He takes it for granted when he sees a good motion picture; he knows the picture is moving smoothly from scene to scene, sequence to sequence, climax to climax.

If the picture, however, moves jerkily, without coherence or flow—*if continuity is lacking*—the moviegoer feels its absence even though he cannot say in so many words what is lacking.

Your audience, your friends, and you will miss it as much whether your picture is for public showing or for personal pleasure.

The fault is the same—and the remedy is the same. You do not use watercolor technique when painting a canvas in oils; it is as illogical to handle a motion-picture camera as though it were a still camera. You cannot have a true motion picture, a good motion picture, without pictorial continuity. That is the answer to the question. It *is* worth it.

A FINAL WORD

You cannot have a good motion picture without pictorial continuity. That is our final word.

That is why we have taken pictorial continuity as the sole subject of this book. Dialogue, music, sound effects, these are familiar adjuncts of the movie of today, but they are grafted on, they are not *inherent motion-picture qualities.* They are aural, not visual qualities.

True, they can be useful, very useful. A motion picture with good continuity can be enhanced by them; but if its continuity is bad or non-existent, aural embellishments are like so much baling wire, desperately —and obviously—used to keep the picture from falling apart. So in this book we have put first things first, and have occupied ourselves exclusively with continuity.

The innate quality of pictorial continuity in a good motion picture is also the reason we have addressed this book not only to anyone who wants to shoot better movies (or just movies that *are* movies), or who has ambitions for writing or directing them, but to the person who wants to *understand* them better as well, whether for his greater enjoyment as a spectator or because he is interested in the motion picture as an art form.

We believe the motion picture to be the greatest medium for story-telling; we believe it offers as rich opportunities for expression as painting or literature. But we also believe it to be a unique medium with a special technique of its own which must be understood.

So to all devotees of the motion picture—ranging from the non-professional who doesn't give a nickel for "art" content but wants to shoot a good home movie of Baby, to the professional critic who has never loaded a camera but is profoundly interested in what a motion picture can say—we urge our variation of the Socratic dictum; it is:

Know your medium—learn pictorial continuity.

ACKNOWLEDGMENTS

The authors wish to acknowledge, with warmest thanks, the valuable criticisms and suggestions of John R. Delaney and Irv Levine, both former staff members of the Army Photographic School; Frank J. Payne, combat photographer and documentary film producer; and Irving Watman, aeronautical engineer and motion-picture enthusiast.

A. L. G.
D. A. E.

CPSIA information can be obtained
at www.ICGtesting.com
Printed in the USA
BVHW030845091222
653835BV00015B/302

9 781258 440008